EYEWITNESS
HURRICANE & TORNADO

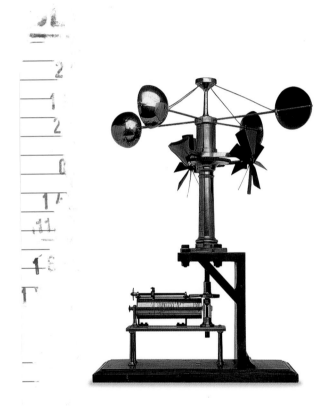

Cyclone shelter

Spots on the Sun

Sunset at Stonehenge, England

19th-century reproduction of Galileo's thermoscope

Saturn

Lighthouse at the George Washington Bridge in New York, USA

Wind-eroded rocks in Utah, USA

Ice crystal

Pine cone's open scales indicate dry weather

EYEWITNESS
HURRICANE & TORNADO

Written by
JACK CHALLONER

Simultaneous waterspout and lightning bolt

Doppler-radar dome

Storm system viewed from space

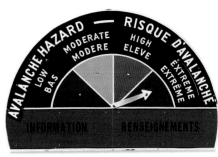

Avalanche-warning sign

LONDON, NEW YORK,
MELBOURNE, MUNICH, AND DELHI

Project editor Melanie Halton
Art editor Ann Cannings
Managing editor Sue Grabham
Senior managing art editor Julia Harris
Editorial consultant Lesley Newson
Picture research Mollie Gillard, Samantha Nunn
DTP designers Andrew O'Brien, Georgia Bryer
Production Kate Oliver

RELAUNCH EDITION (DK UK)
Editor Ashwin Khurana
Senior designers Rachael Grady, Spencer Holbrook
Managing editor Gareth Jones
Managing art editor Philip Letsu
Publisher Andrew Macintyre
Producer, pre-production Adam Stoneham
Senior producer Charlotte Cade
Jacket editor Manisha Majithia, Maud Whatley
Jacket designer Laura Brim
Jacket design development manager Sophia MTT
Publishing director Jonathan Metcalf
Associate publishing director Liz Wheeler
Art director Phil Ormerod

RELAUNCH EDITION (DK INDIA)
Senior editor Neha Gupta
Art editors Deep Shikha Walia, Shreya Sadhan
Senior DTP designer Harish Aggarwal
DTP designer Pawan Kumar
Managing editor Alka Thakur Hazarika
Managing art editor Romi Chakraborty
CTS manager Balwant Singh
Jacket editorial manager Saloni Talwar
Jacket designers Vidit Vashisht

This Eyewitness ® Guide has been conceived by
Dorling Kindersley Limited and Editions Gallimard

First published in Great Britain in 1995
This relaunch edition published in 2014 by
Dorling Kindersley Limited, 80 Strand, London WC2R 0RL

Copyright © 1995, © 2003, © 2008, © 2014
Dorling Kindersley Limited
A Penguin Random House Company

2 4 6 8 10 9 7 5 3 1
196431 – 07/14

A CIP catalogue record for this book is
available from the British Library.
ISBN 978-1-4093-4376-9

Colour reproduction by Alta Image Ltd, London, UK
Printed and bound by South China Printing Co Ltd, China

Discover more at

www.dk.com

Venetian blind twisted by a tornado

Storm erupts on the Sun

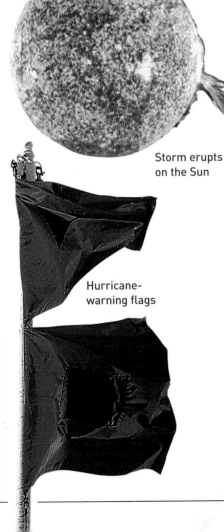

Hurricane-warning flags

Italian thermometer (1657)

Contents

Icicle formation
in Arizona, USA

Weather folklore

In ancient times, people didn't know how the weather worked. Some realized that clouds were made of water, but they did not understand the wind or the Sun. Many believed the gods made the weather; others observed plants, animals, or the sky to deduce a forecast. Some of these observations were reliable, but an accurate forecast requires a full understanding of how the weather works. Weather science was begun by philosophers in ancient Greece, but they did not test their theories, and so they were often wrong.

Cone watch
Pine cones open their scales in dry air and close them when it is humid. Air is normally humid before rainfall, so pine cones can help forecast wet weather.

Italian fresco showing Plato and Aristotle (1511)

Thinkers
Ancient Greek philosophers Aristotle and Plato were among the first people to try to explain scientifically how the weather works, including cloud, hail, storm, and snow formation, plus Sun haloes. Their ideas were very influential and were not challenged for about 2,000 years

Rain cry
These Yali tribesmen of New Guinea are performing a dance to call for rain. Dancers carry grass, which is believed to pierce the eye of the Sun and makes it cry tears of rain.

Animal forecast
Many animals respond to changes in temperature, humidity, or atmospheric pressure, such as cocks, which often crow before a thunderstorm. Observing animals can help with weather forecasts.

Sun worship

Throughout history, many cultures have worshipped the Sun. Stonehenge in England is thought to be an ancient place of Sun worship. Some stones line up to where the Sun rises on the summer solstice (when the Sun is at its highest).

Stonehenge was built between 3000 BCE and 1500 BCE

Sky watching

An ancient Maori myth describes Tawhaki, the god of thunder and lightning, going up to the sky disguised as a kite. Maori priests believed they could predict the weather by flying kites and watching how they moved across the sky.

Maori kite made of canvas and twigs

Magic charms

This figurehead from the Solomon Islands would have been on the front of a canoe to ward off dangerous storms at sea. Many lucky charms that are used to protect people against bad weather are linked to gods or spirits.

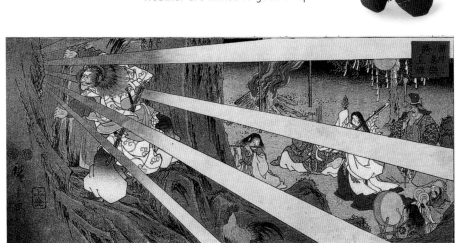

Stormy tale

In the Shinto religion, divine being Amaterasu Omikami lights up heaven. Her brother, a storm god, causes strong winds and floods, which make Amaterasu hide in a cave and the world go dark – just like during a storm.

Statue of Chac, Mayan rain god

Weather sacrifice

Legend says that the Mayan rain god, Chac, sent rain for crops, but also storms, which destroyed crops. People made offerings to Chac to keep the rains but stop the storms.

Furry tale

Some people believe that the bushier a squirrel's tail is during autumn, the harsher the winter will be. There is no scientific evidence for this.

Bushy tailed squirrel

Early forecasts

Meteorology, or modern weather science, began about 300 years ago when people started to experiment scientifically with water, heat, and air – the components of weather. They learnt about atmospheric pressure, the gases of air, and water evaporation. Early meteorologists invented crude measuring devices to test theories. Important developments were the barometer (measures atmospheric pressure), the thermometer (measures temperature), and hygrometer (measures humidity). Today, sophisticated equipment allows accurate predictions of extreme weather.

Glass bulb

Under pressure

In 1643, Italian physicist Evangelista Torricelli made the first barometer – a 1-m- (3-ft-) long tube filled with mercury and put upside down in a bowl of mercury. The weight, or pressure, of air on the mercury in the bowl stopped the mercury in the tube from falling below 76 cm (30 in).

Moving mercury

Meteorologist Robert Fitzroy invented this barometer, which has a scale to measure the mercury column. Fine weather is forecast when atmospheric pressure pushes the mercury column above 76 cm (30 in); unsettled weather is predicted when it falls below this.

Fitzroy barometer

High temperature

Italian physicist Galileo Galilei designed this thermoscope (early thermometer) about 400 years ago. A long tube with a bulb at the end sat in a flask of water. As the temperature rose, air in the bulb expanded, causing the water level in the tube to drop. As it became cooler, the air contracted and the water level rose.

Flask would have been filled with water

Cotton bag for absorbing moisture in the air

Invisible water

Air normally becomes humid (contains more water) before a thunderstorm. The water in the air is an invisible vapour, but a hygrometer, designed about 350 years ago, is able to measure it. Water is absorbed from the air by the cotton bag, which becomes heavier. The greater the humidity, the more the bag drops down.

Balancing weight made of glass

A 19th-century reproduction of Galileo's original thermoscope

17th-century balance hygrometer

When the water level in the spout is high, air pressure is low, and storms can be expected

When working, the level of water in the weather glass would have been much higher

Weather glass

In this simple barometer, atmospheric pressure pushes down on the water in the sealed flask arm. The air inside the arm pushes in the other direction. As atmospheric pressure changes, the water level rises and falls. Before a storm, air pressure drops, and the water rises up the arm.

Image of Sun is reflected in the glass orb

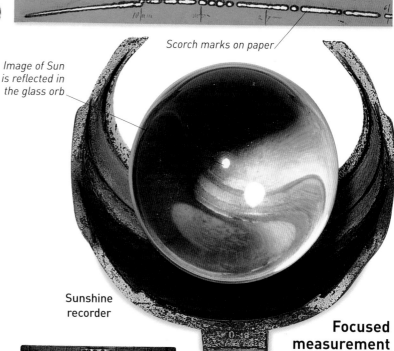

Scorch marks on paper

Sunshine recorder

Focused measurement

This glass ball focuses sunlight to scorch paper. As the Sun moves across the sky, the trail of scorches shows the amount of sunlight. If clouds hide the Sun, there is not enough direct sunlight to scorch paper.

Thick needle aligns with the normal path of storms in the region

Thin needle indicates safe course away from the storm

Hotness scale

When this thermometer was made, in 1657, there was no agreed scale for reading measurements. Today, meteorologists use two main scales to record temperature – Celsius and Fahrenheit. Both scales were invented in the 18th century.

Ornate thermometer made in Italy, 1657

An eye on the storm

Cyclonic winds spiral at their centre, and so, before hurricane radio warnings, sailors used this barocyclonometer to measure changes in wind direction and atmospheric pressure. They could then work out which way the hurricane was moving and steer their vessels to safety.

A hotty

The spiralling tube of this glass thermometer saves space. When the temperature increases, water in the lower bulb expands, filling more of the spiral tube. The higher the water in the tube, the higher the temperature.

It's a gas

During the 1770s, French chemist Antoine Lavoisier was the first person to discover that the atmosphere is a mixture of gases. He also found that hydrogen and oxygen combine to make water.

What is extreme weather?

From hurricanes and tornadoes, droughts and floods to freezing and high temperatures, extreme weather can be dangerous. Weather can be described by wind speed, temperature, atmospheric pressure, and precipitation (rain, hail, or snow). The average world temperature is 15°C (59°F), but some places are colder or warmer. The average rainfall is 100 cm (39 in) per year, but some places have no rain, others too much and all at once. Extreme weather can happen where weather is usually calm.

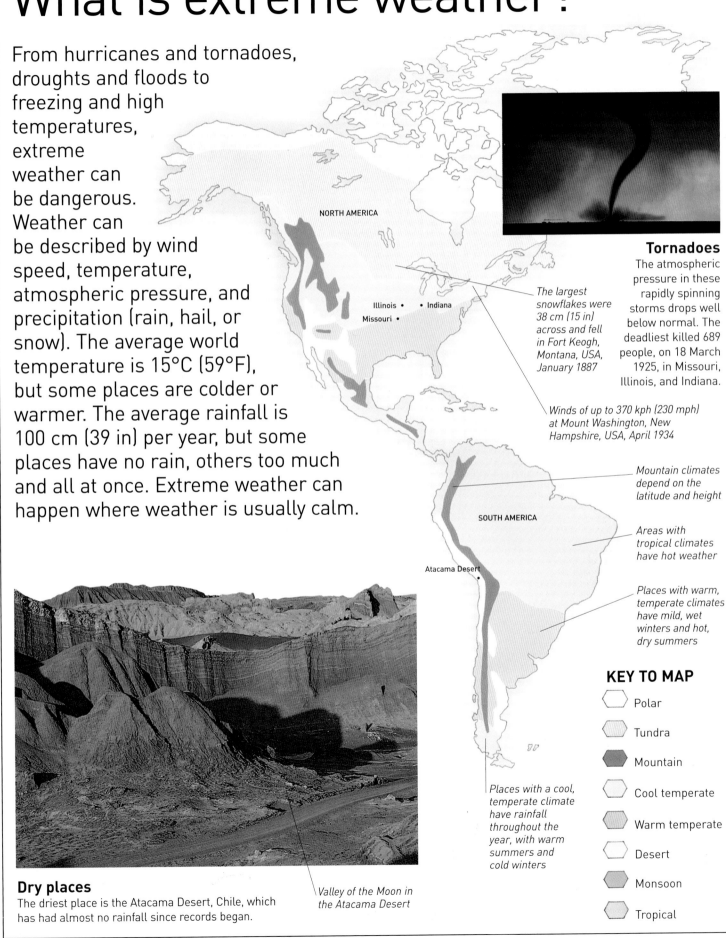

NORTH AMERICA

Illinois •   • Indiana
Missouri •

SOUTH AMERICA

Atacama Desert

Tornadoes
The atmospheric pressure in these rapidly spinning storms drops well below normal. The deadliest killed 689 people, on 18 March 1925, in Missouri, Illinois, and Indiana.

The largest snowflakes were 38 cm (15 in) across and fell in Fort Keogh, Montana, USA, January 1887

Winds of up to 370 kph (230 mph) at Mount Washington, New Hampshire, USA, April 1934

Mountain climates depend on the latitude and height

Areas with tropical climates have hot weather

Places with warm, temperate climates have mild, wet winters and hot, dry summers

Places with a cool, temperate climate have rainfall throughout the year, with warm summers and cold winters

KEY TO MAP

⬡ Polar

⬡ Tundra

⬡ Mountain

⬡ Cool temperate

⬡ Warm temperate

⬡ Desert

⬡ Monsoon

⬡ Tropical

Dry places
The driest place is the Atacama Desert, Chile, which has had almost no rainfall since records began.

Valley of the Moon in the Atacama Desert

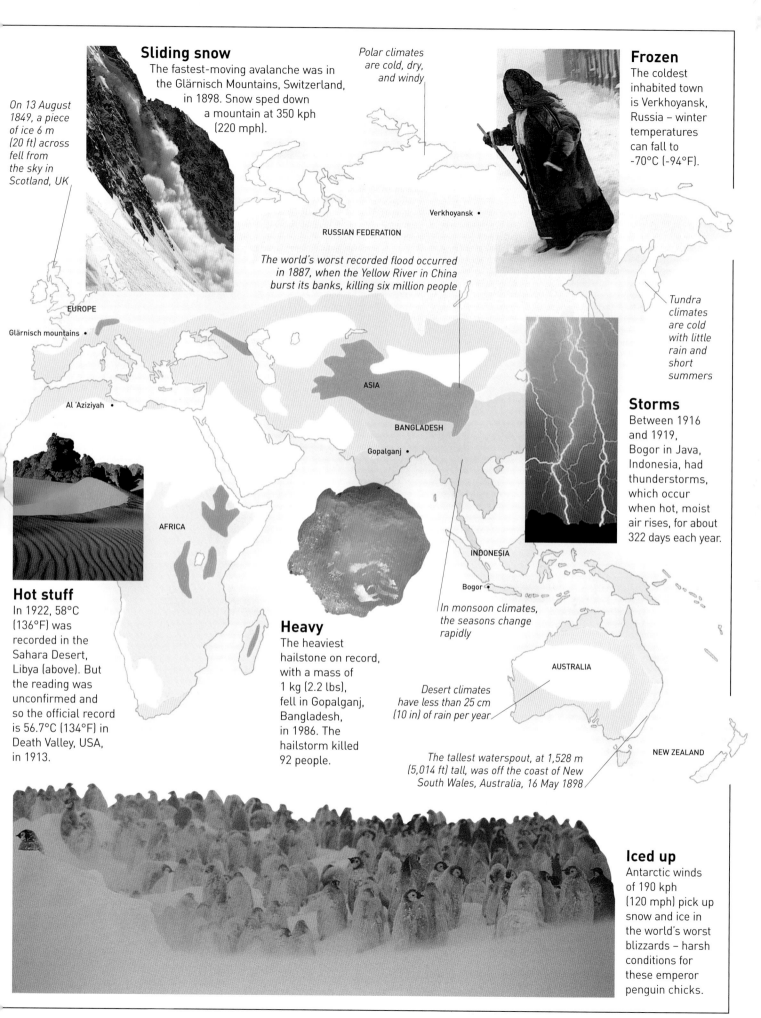

Sliding snow
The fastest-moving avalanche was in the Glärnisch Mountains, Switzerland, in 1898. Snow sped down a mountain at 350 kph (220 mph).

Polar climates are cold, dry, and windy

Frozen
The coldest inhabited town is Verkhoyansk, Russia – winter temperatures can fall to -70°C (-94°F).

On 13 August 1849, a piece of ice 6 m (20 ft) across fell from the sky in Scotland, UK

Verkhoyansk •

RUSSIAN FEDERATION

The world's worst recorded flood occurred in 1887, when the Yellow River in China burst its banks, killing six million people

EUROPE

Glärnisch mountains •

ASIA

BANGLADESH

Gopalganj •

Tundra climates are cold with little rain and short summers

Storms
Between 1916 and 1919, Bogor in Java, Indonesia, had thunderstorms, which occur when hot, moist air rises, for about 322 days each year.

Al 'Aziziyah •

AFRICA

INDONESIA

Bogor •

In monsoon climates, the seasons change rapidly

Hot stuff
In 1922, 58°C (136°F) was recorded in the Sahara Desert, Libya (above). But the reading was unconfirmed and so the official record is 56.7°C (134°F) in Death Valley, USA, in 1913.

Heavy
The heaviest hailstone on record, with a mass of 1 kg (2.2 lbs), fell in Gopalganj, Bangladesh, in 1986. The hailstorm killed 92 people.

Desert climates have less than 25 cm (10 in) of rain per year

AUSTRALIA

The tallest waterspout, at 1,528 m (5,014 ft) tall, was off the coast of New South Wales, Australia, 16 May 1898

NEW ZEALAND

Iced up
Antarctic winds of 190 kph (120 mph) pick up snow and ice in the world's worst blizzards – harsh conditions for these emperor penguin chicks.

Extreme causes

Important factors that affect the weather include the Sun heating Earth and differences in atmospheric pressure. Other factors include dust from volcanoes and storms on the Sun's surface, which can make it hotter or colder, wetter or drier. Pollution in the atmosphere also affects the weather. Causes of extreme weather are understood, but predicting weather more than a few days ahead is still impossible because the weather is a complex and sensitive system.

Chaotic weather
According to chaos theory – the study of unpredictable systems – a butterfly can change the course of the weather; it is so sensitive to atmospheric conditions that a slight change in air movement, such as by a flapping wing, can alter the course of the world's weather.

Spotting bad weather
Dark, cool patches can appear on the Sun's surface for about a week. These sunspots throw out debris that sometimes reach Earth. The spots are most numerous every 11 years, and extreme weather on Earth seems to coincide with this cycle.

Global warming
Many gases and smoke particles from modern industry hang in the air. This can affect the weather. Carbon dioxide from fossil fuels is contributing to an increase in the world's temperature. This "global warming" could upset weather balances, bringing more storms and rising sea levels.

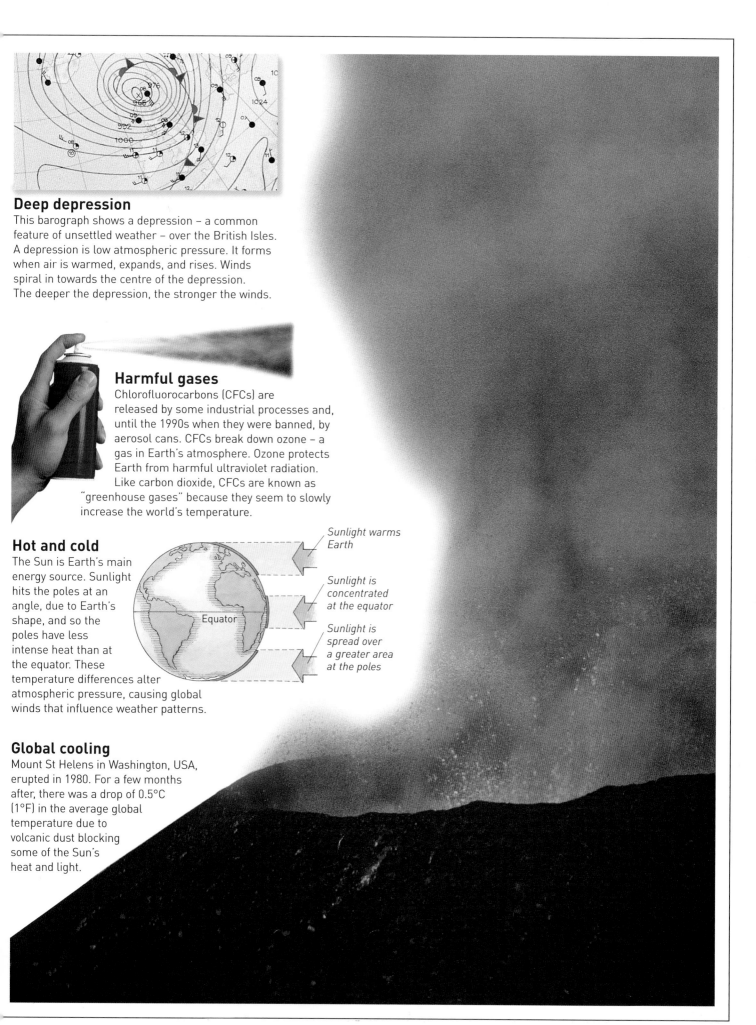

Deep depression

This barograph shows a depression – a common feature of unsettled weather – over the British Isles. A depression is low atmospheric pressure. It forms when air is warmed, expands, and rises. Winds spiral in towards the centre of the depression. The deeper the depression, the stronger the winds.

Harmful gases

Chlorofluorocarbons (CFCs) are released by some industrial processes and, until the 1990s when they were banned, by aerosol cans. CFCs break down ozone – a gas in Earth's atmosphere. Ozone protects Earth from harmful ultraviolet radiation. Like carbon dioxide, CFCs are known as "greenhouse gases" because they seem to slowly increase the world's temperature.

Hot and cold

The Sun is Earth's main energy source. Sunlight hits the poles at an angle, due to Earth's shape, and so the poles have less intense heat than at the equator. These temperature differences alter atmospheric pressure, causing global winds that influence weather patterns.

Equator

Sunlight warms Earth

Sunlight is concentrated at the equator

Sunlight is spread over a greater area at the poles

Global cooling

Mount St Helens in Washington, USA, erupted in 1980. For a few months after, there was a drop of 0.5°C (1°F) in the average global temperature due to volcanic dust blocking some of the Sun's heat and light.

Severe winds

Strong winds can wreak havoc. Their force depends on their speed. The fastest winds at ground level are in hurricanes and tornadoes; higher in the atmosphere are even faster winds – jet streams – that help to distribute the Sun's heat around the world. Global winds are caused by the Sun heating parts of the Earth differently, while local winds are caused by regional changes in temperature and pressure.

All at sea
In 1805, British naval commander Francis Beaufort devised a system for estimating wind speeds at sea. The Beaufort Scale assigns names and numbers to 12 different strengths of wind. It is still used today.

Standing tall
This model shows the 840-m (2,755-ft) tall Millennium Tower proposed for Tokyo, Japan. An important feature for a skyscraper is wind resistance. This tower is encircled by a steel frame to strengthen it and protect it from winds.

Architectural model of **Millennium Tower, Tokyo**

Head faces in the direction from which the wind is blowing

Weather vane
Weather vanes are perhaps the oldest meteorological instruments. This weather cock's tail swings around as the wind changes direction, and points the head towards the wind. A reading is taken of where the wind blows from.

Flying in the wind
In March 1999, balloonists Bertrand Piccard and Brian Jones became the first to fly a hot-air balloon nonstop around the world. Their balloon, *Breitling Orbiter 3*, was sometimes assisted by jet-stream winds, blowing up to 300 kph (186 mph).

Wind swept
Wind and sand erosion has carved these sandstone rocks. If severe winds blow across the rocks, sweeping up sand, dense and dangerous sandstorms may occur.

Wind vane to show direction

Cups spin around – their speed depends on wind strength

Rotors turn wind vane into the wind

Average wind speed is recorded as the cylinder rotates

Wind recorder
This anemometer records wind speed and direction over a period of time. To understand how the wind works, forecasters need to take as many measurements as possible.

Weathered sandstone, Colorado Plateau, Utah, USA

A man struggles on Chicago's Wabash Avenue Bridge in fierce winds

The windy city
Chicago, USA, is near the Great Lakes, where inland and lake air mix. The atmospheric pressure of these air masses is different, and so winds batter Chicago as they collide.

Swing bridge
Strong gusts caused the Tacoma Narrows Bridge in Washington, USA, to swing in 1940. Eventually, the bridge collapsed. Since the winds were not hurricane strength, the bridge's design was blamed.

Thunderous storms

Huge amounts of energy are released in the rain, winds, thunder, and lightning that accompany thunderstorms. The most energetic storms create hail or tornadoes. The source of energy is the Sun, which causes water to evaporate; the resulting warm, moist air rises and cools, creating a cumulonimbus cloud. The rising current of air (an updraught) may travel more than 100 kph (60 mph). When rain or hail falls, a downdraught of cooler air causes gusty winds.

Letting go
Tornadoes, lightning, and waterspouts often occur during severe storms as thunderclouds quickly release energy.

View from the air
This photograph, taken from a spacecraft orbiting Earth, shows how a system of storms can develop when cold, dry air undercuts warm, moist air, lifting it to form pockets of rising air. These pockets show up as thunderheads.

Water carrier
A thunderhead is a towering cumulonimbus cloud. It may reach a height of 12 km (7.5 miles), while its base may loom just 1,000 m (3,280 ft) above ground. It usually contains about 10,000 tonnes (11,023 US tons) of water.

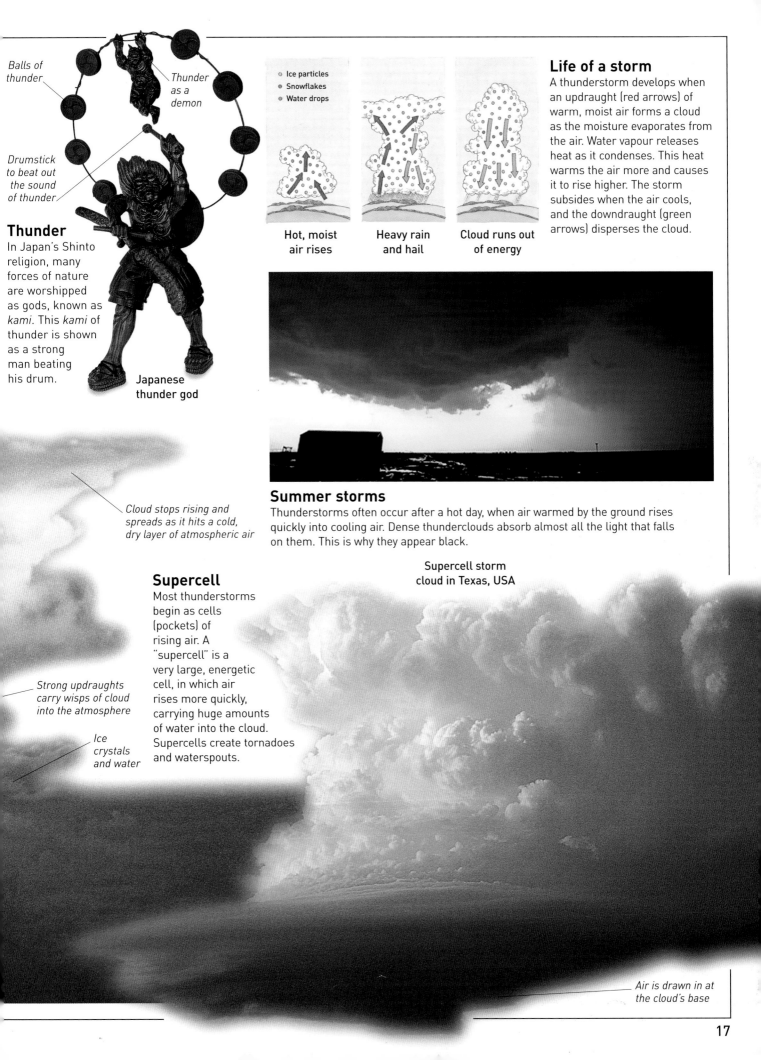

Thunder

Balls of thunder

Thunder as a demon

Drumstick to beat out the sound of thunder

In Japan's Shinto religion, many forces of nature are worshipped as gods, known as *kami*. This *kami* of thunder is shown as a strong man beating his drum.

Japanese thunder god

Life of a storm

- Ice particles
- Snowflakes
- Water drops

A thunderstorm develops when an updraught (red arrows) of warm, moist air forms a cloud as the moisture evaporates from the air. Water vapour releases heat as it condenses. This heat warms the air more and causes it to rise higher. The storm subsides when the air cools, and the downdraught (green arrows) disperses the cloud.

Hot, moist air rises

Heavy rain and hail

Cloud runs out of energy

Summer storms

Thunderstorms often occur after a hot day, when air warmed by the ground rises quickly into cooling air. Dense thunderclouds absorb almost all the light that falls on them. This is why they appear black.

Supercell storm cloud in Texas, USA

Cloud stops rising and spreads as it hits a cold, dry layer of atmospheric air

Supercell

Strong updraughts carry wisps of cloud into the atmosphere

Ice crystals and water

Most thunderstorms begin as cells (pockets) of rising air. A "supercell" is a very large, energetic cell, in which air rises more quickly, carrying huge amounts of water into the cloud. Supercells create tornadoes and waterspouts.

Air is drawn in at the cloud's base

Twisting tornadoes

Tornadoes have many names, including whirlwinds and twisters. These high-speed spiralling winds leave a trail of destruction and are a bit of a mystery. They seem to develop at the base of thunderclouds as warm, moist air rises and passes through colder air. Somehow this draws winds that are already circulating the storm into a high-speed whirl. The pressure at a tornado's centre is lower than outside, creating a funnel that sucks up anything in its path.

A tornado funnel appears at the base of a thundercloud

1 Wall of cloud
These photographs show how a tornado develops. Its funnel descends from a thundercloud above. A column of cloud then forms as moisture as the air condenses in the low pressure inside the tornado.

Swirling black thundercloud indicates the start of a tornado

Funnel changes colour as it picks up debris

2 Down to earth
This tornado is passing over dusty farmland. The base of the tornado is therefore obscured by dust picked up by the rising air and swirling winds.

Liquid funnel
When a tornado passes over water, the updraught at its centre sucks up water, forming a water-spout. A waterspout's wind speeds are much less than in ordinary tornadoes due to the weight of the water it carries.

Funnel narrows as the tornado's energy diminishes

3 Losing power
Energy from the tornado's winds throws debris into the air. As the tornado loses energy, it slows down. The funnel will then shrink back to the thundercloud from which it was born.

Animal rain
When a tornado passes over water, small animals may be lifted into the air, only to rain down once the tornado loses its energy.

Spin cycle
The writhing funnel of rapidly spinning air descends to the ground from the base of a supercell. At a tornado's heart, a low-pressure vortex acts like a huge vacuum cleaner, sucking up air and anything on the ground.

Kicking up dust
Dust devils are common in desert regions. Although less energetic and less destructive than tornadoes, they are created in the same way. The circling winds typically reach speeds of about 40 kph (25 mph).

Tornado force

The swirling winds of a tornado are among the most destructive forces in nature, with speeds of up to 500 kph (310 mph). A violent tornado will destroy everything in its path. Most of the world's destructive tornadoes occur during summer in mid-west USA, where cold air from Canada in the north sits atop warm, moist air from the Gulf of Mexico to the south. This region is often called Tornado Alley. Predicting where and when tornadoes will occur is extremely difficult.

Towering

The destructive vortex (spinning centre) of a tornado is usually about 2 km (1 mile) wide. Dust or objects at ground level are lifted high into the air and flung sideways, or kept in the air and deposited when the tornado winds down. Tornadoes typically travel at 55 kph (34 mph).

Venetian blind twisted by a tornado

Tornado funnel descends from a thundercloud

Blind panic

Much of a tornado's destruction is caused by the sudden drop in pressure that it brings. This window exploded outwards when a tornado went by because air pressure inside the room was higher than outside.

Door sucked out of a window by the tornado's force

Tornado Alley

This map shows the area in the USA known as Tornado Alley, which includes parts of Kansas, Oklahoma, and Missouri. It experiences several hundred tornadoes every year; they claim about 100 lives each year in the USA.

CANADA

UNITED STATES

Kansas · · Missouri
· Oklahoma

MEXICO

Areas most at risk from tornadoes

Blown away

In March 1994, a torndado ripped the roof off this church in Piedmont, Virginia, USA, surprising the congregation during a service.

In a twist

Tornado winds travelling at more than 400 kph (250 mph) picked up this truck and hurled it down again, leaving behind a mess of twisted steel and showing the incredible power of a tornado.

Dust and debris are swept up as the tornado moves along

Swirling vortex

Twisting column of cloud

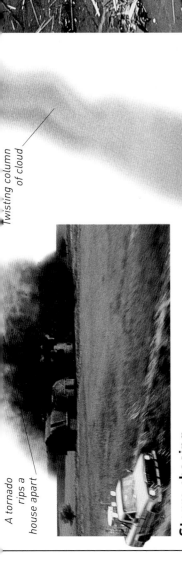

A tornado rips a house apart

Storm chasing

In the USA, storm chasers pursue tornadoes to learn more about them when a "tornado watch" warning is issued.

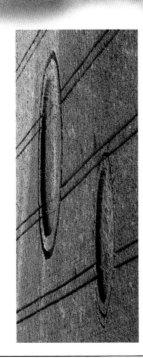

Circles of mystery

For centuries, unexplained circles of flattened crops have appeared in fields across the world. Some people believe that tornadoes are responsible, but this is unlikely since tornadoes do not hover over one spot for long enough.

Strange tales

A chicken in Alabama, USA, is reported to have survived tornadic winds of about 200 kph (124 mph), which stripped it of its tail and feathers.

Measuring tornadoes

Meteorologists use an anemometer to accurately measure wind speeds, but getting one inside a tornado is dangerous, and, because tornadoes move, it is difficult to get accurate readings. And so meteorologists categorized tornadoes based on estimated wind speed and damage caused. Today, though, the Doppler weather radar accurately measures wind speeds inside a tornado.

Path of a tornado
Most tornadoes travel at 30–80 kph (20–50 mph). This image shows the path of devastation left by a tornado in Oklahoma, USA, in 1999.

Radar dish sends out and receives microwaves

Doppler on wheels
Doppler radar, mounted on a truck to get close to the tornado, measures wind speed in a tornado without equipment breaking or anybody getting hurt. Microwaves directed at the tornado's edge bounce off water droplets carried by the wind. Computers in the truck then work out the speed at which the droplets are moving.

NCAR

DOW3

DOPPLER ON WHEELS

Tetsuya (Ted) Fujita (1920–1998)

In 1971, this severe weather expert designed the Fujita (F) Scale, which categorizes tornadoes based on the damage they cause. Today, most countries use the Enhanced Fujita (EF) Scale. Meteorologists in Britain use the TORRO (T) Scale.

Portable TOTO

Now defunct, the TOtable (meaning portable) Tornado Observatory (TOTO) was a metal drum containing instruments, which could be placed in the path of approaching tornadoes. After many failed attempts, researchers finally got it right in 1984, but TOTO was blown over by just a moderate tornado.

Enhanced Fujita Scale

Meteorologists in the USA and Canada began using the Enhanced Fujita (EF) Scale, which runs from EF0 to EF5, in 2007. Several other countries also use it. It gives more accurate wind speed estimates.

EF0: Minor Damage
The 105–137 kph (65–85 mph) winds can uproot shallow-rooted trees and damage chimneys.

EF1: Moderate Damage
Moderate winds of 138–177 kph (86–110 mph) overturn mobile homes, damage roofs and windows.

EF2: Considerable Damage
The 178–217 kph (111–135 mph) winds can tear off roofs, uproot large trees, and lift cars off the ground.

EF3: Severe Damage
Intense 218–266 kph (136–165 mph) winds damage well-constructed buildings, and can overturn trains.

EF4: Devastating Damage
Wind speeds of 267–322 kph (166–200 mph) can ruin houses, and lift cars, blowing them long distances.

EF5: Incredible Damage
Wind speeds of more than 322 kph (200 mph) are very rare but are able to detach houses from their foundations.

Lightning strikes

Nearly 2,000 thunderstorms occur at any one time across Earth. Their most impressive feature is lightning, caused by an electric charge that builds up inside a thundercloud. Air inside the cloud rises at speeds of up to 100 kph (60 mph) and carries tiny ice crystals to the top of the cloud. These rub against hail pellets as they rise. The ice crystals become positively charged; the hail becomes negatively charged. A lightning bolt is simply a huge spark that neutralizes the electric charges.

Stormy god
Before scientists explained weather patterns, many cultures believed weather to be controlled by gods. The Norse god Thor was believed to make thunderbolts with his hammer.

Fossilized lightning bolt

Sand sculpture
This fossil is sand that has melted and then solidified in the path of a typical 30,000°C (54,000°F) bolt of lightning. The resulting mineral is fulgurite.

Bright spark
During a storm in 1752, American politician and scientist Benjamin Franklin flew a kite with metal items on its string. Sparks from the items showed electricity had passed along the wet string.

Personal safety
The Franklin wire was invented by Benjamin Franklin in 1753. The metallic wire, hung from a hat or umbrella, dragged on the ground to divert lightning from the wearer.

Lightning conductors were all the rage in Paris, 1778

Lightning rods
Tall buildings, such as the Eiffel Tower in Paris, France, are regularly hit by lightning. Metal rods (called lightning conductors) attached to the buildings conduct the electricity to the ground.

This tree has been torn apart by lightning

Quick as a flash

Lightning, such as the successive flashes of this storm, begins as a "leader stroke" at the base of a thundercloud, and forms a path of charged atoms. Electric charges race along this path, producing a bright glow and making the air heat up rapidly and expand. This creates a shockwave – a loud thunderclap.

Cloud illuminated from within by a lightning bolt

Lightning force

The power of lightning can demolish a building or kill a person or animal. Trees are vulnerable to lightning strikes because the moist layer below the bark acts as a conductor.

Sky lights

Most lightning bolts occur within a cloud. A powerful electric current passes between the positively charged top of the cloud and its negatively charged base.

Hailstorms

Balls of ice called hailstones are produced inside a thundercloud. The strong air currents force lumps of ice up and down the cloud. With each upward movement the hailstones collect another layer of ice, until they are too big to be lifted again by the up-currents. The stronger the up-current, the heavier a hailstone can become. Heavy hailstones can be life-threatening, but any hailstorm can cause damage. One of the worst storms was in Munich, Germany, in July 1984, with financial losses around £625 million ($1 billion).

Combating hail in cotton fields in the Fergana Valley, Russia

Cloud bursting

To save their crops from hail damage, the Russians fire chemical substances into thunderclouds, making potential hail fall as harmless rain. This has saved vast prairies of grain that could otherwise have been flattened by hail within minutes.

Heavy storm

Hailstones are usually about the size of a pea. They bounce when they hit a hard surface, and tend to settle on the ground. But hailstones vary in size, and storms in severity. In the USA alone, a hailstorm can cause property damage of more than £300 million ($500 million), and crop damage of £185 million ($300 million).

Maize crop destroyed by a severe hailstorm

Hail Alley

A belt of land in the USA, spanning from Texas to Montana, is known as "Hail Alley" and regularly experiences severe hailstorms. Little has been done in the USA to explore methods of crop protection, though.

Vehicles pelted by hail during a storm in Texas, USA, in May 1977

Dangerous driving

Driving through a hailstorm is hazardous; vehicles skid on the hard, icy stones. The damage caused by falling hail depends on the wind speed during a storm. Hailstones with a diameter of 10 cm (4 in) travel at speeds of up to 170 kph (106 mph).

Windscreen shattered by a hailstone during a storm near Burlington, Colorado, USA, in 1990

This hailstone is the size of a grapefruit

Ice pack

Hailstones are made up of layers – a bit like onions. Each layer represents one journey through the cloud in which it formed. This hailstone – one of the largest ever found – had a diameter of 19 cm (7.5 in), and a mass of 766 g (1.67 lbs).

Cross-section of a hailstone

Big chill

Large hailstones usually fall from "supercell" thunderclouds, which typically have a very strong updraught. This 10-cm (4-in) diameter hailstone fell in Colorado, USA, in May 1978.

Drivers park their vehicles at the side of the road as they wait for the danger to pass

Hurricane alert

Hurricanes, or tropical cyclones, are also known as cyclones in the Indian Ocean, and typhoons in the Pacific. They are huge, rotating storms with winds of up to 350 kph (217 mph), heavy rain, and stormy seas. In the warm seas of the tropics (near the equator), a hurricane begins as heated air expands and rises, creating an area of low pressure. Surrounding air moves towards the low pressure, and spins due to Earth's rotation.

Warning

The destruction from a hurricane can be reduced if a warning is given. These flags are a hurricane alert.

Many buildings were wrecked when a cyclone hit Albany, Georgia, USA in 1940

Gale force

The destructive force of a hurricane comes largely from its strong winds. As more and more air is drawn in towards the centre of the storm, the spiralling winds' speed increases.

19th-century aneroid barometer

Under pressure

The atmospheric pressure, measured by a barometer, is very low in a hurricane. Changes in pressure can help predict approaching storms.

Wheeled warning

In a Bangladesh village, where few people have radios or televisions, this man is using a megaphone to warn of a hurricane.

Water, water...

Under the low pressure air at the centre of a storm, the sea level bulges to as much as 1 m (3 ft) higher than normal. This "storm surge" adds to the flooding along coastlines, which causes most of the deaths from hurricanes.

A community in Bangladesh waits for a hurricane threat to pass

Stilts raise this purpose-built cyclone shelter above the ground

Safety on stilts

Floods are common during a hurricane, from heavy rains and high ocean waves. This shelter is raised so that flood waters can pass beneath it without endangering lives.

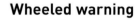

Spinning cyclones

Hurricanes are tropical cyclones.
A cyclone is an area of low-pressure
air with winds that spiral inwards –
clockwise in the southern
hemisphere, anti-clockwise in
the northern. They move west
from their origin near the
equator, but may curve
back east as they
cross the tropics.

Northern
hemisphere

Equator

NEW
GUINEA

AUSTRALIA

Southern
hemisphere

View from above

Hurricanes form where the sea water is above
27°C (80°F). A low pressure forms. Once winds
reach 62 kph (39 mph), it is a tropical storm.
When they reach 118 kph (74 mph), it is
a hurricane and picks up 2 billion tonnes
(2.2 billion US tons) of water, as vapour,
from the ocean each day. This vapour
condenses to form clouds. The eye,
or centre, of a hurricane is very
calm, while all around it are thick
clouds and high-speed winds.

*The eye of a storm
can be up to 50 km
(31 miles) wide*

**Satellite
view of
Hurricane
Emilia (1994)**

Devastation

Some regions are more prone to hurricanes than others. Areas outside the tropics – more than 2,500 km (1,550 miles) from the equator – are much less at risk than tropical regions because the seas are cooler, providing less energy to fuel hurricanes. Hurricanes bring huge waves, known as storm surges, which cause the biggest loss of lives. But it is the strong winds that cause the greatest destruction.

The hurricane of 1900 demolished this school in Galveston, but the desks are still screwed to the floor

American tragedy
One of the deadliest hurricanes in the USA struck the coastal city of Galveston, Texas, in September 1900. More than 12,000 people died, 2,600 homes were destroyed, and about 10,000 people were left homeless.

Hurricane David's powerful winds lifted this plane and deposited it on top of a hangar

Hanging around
The Dominican Republic was struck by dangerous and destructive Hurricane David in August 1979. The storm reached speeds of 277 kph (172 mph), and lasted two weeks, bombarding the coastline with huge waves; 1,300 people lost their lives.

In the bunker

Flood waters produced by Hurricane Hugo in 1989 swept this boat from the harbour to a nearby golf course. Hugo hit the Virgin Islands before moving over warm water, where it gained energy, and struck South Carolina, USA.

A low, flat, and well-secured roof helped this house to survive almost entirely intact

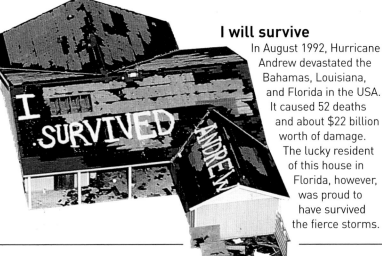

Reduced to rubble

In April 1991, Cyclone 2B hit Bangladesh; 240-kph (150-mph) winds reduced homes to rubble, and a 6-m (20-ft) tidal wave claimed more than 140,000 lives.

Wave power

Due to low atmospheric pressure at a hurricane's heart, there is a swell of water up to 3 m (10 ft) high. If it moves close to land, the swell becomes a huge wave, flooding vast areas, such as when Hurricane Floyd struck the USA in 1999.

Without warning

In late December 1974, Cyclone Tracy formed 500 km (310 miles) northeast of the Australian coast. The local Tropical Cyclone Warning Centre suggested the hurricane would miss land, but early on Christmas Day, it turned and hit Darwin. About 90 per cent of the buildings were destroyed, leaving half of its 40,000 people homeless; more than 20,000 people were airlifted out.

I will survive

In August 1992, Hurricane Andrew devastated the Bahamas, Louisiana, and Florida in the USA. It caused 52 deaths and about $22 billion worth of damage. The lucky resident of this house in Florida, however, was proud to have survived the fierce storms.

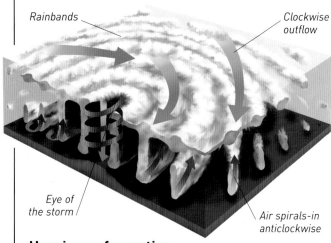

Rainbands

Clockwise outflow

Eye of the storm

Air spirals-in anticlockwise

Hurricane formation

Hurricanes develop above warm ocean waters. Moist, rising air causes an area of very low pressure. Surrounding air spirals inwards and forms curved clouds called rainbands. Air from the eye (centre) flows out above the storm.

Hurricane strikes

It usually takes several days for storms over tropical oceans to develop into hurricanes. By studying how hurricanes develop, meteorologists can better predict which storm will become a hurricane, where it is likely to go, and how powerful it might be, helping emergency services to better prepare, and giving people more time to evacuate.

Centre of the storm is a low-pressure area

1 Hurricane trigger

These satellite images show Hurricane Katrina's development in 2005. The storm began forming on 23 August, in warm waters over the Bahamas. A centre of low pressure began drawing in air.

Gusty winds

This picture shows the conditions beneath a hurricane's spiralling clouds. The high winds are caused by huge differences in atmospheric pressure. As the air spirals inwards, it speeds up.

Trees bend over in the strong wind

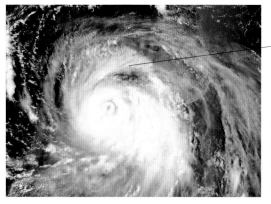

Rainbands form as air swirls in towards the centre

2 A swirling mass

The storm absorbed more energy from the warm water in the Gulf of Mexico, and formed huge spiral rainbands. On 25 August, it moved northwest and passed over Florida, USA, and back into the Gulf.

Hurricane's eye is calm

3 Mature stage

By 29 August, the storm had a well-defined eye. It hit land again in Louisiana, USA, where flooding and high winds caused damage worth billions of dollars.

Hurricane reader

Mounted on aircraft that fly over storm clouds, the High-Altitude Imaging Wind and Rain Airborne Profiler (HIWRAP) uses radar to measure wind speeds around hurricanes, which helps scientists understand and make more accurate predictions about these storms.

Dish reflector

Two "transceivers" transmit and receive radar beams

Flood-ridden New Orleans

Hurricane Katrina was the costliest and one of the five most deadly hurricanes in US history. Almost 2,000 people died, and damage costs were at least $81 billion. The worst-hit area was New Orleans, where the storm surge – a bulge of sea water – poured over the levees (flood barriers).

Hurricane Wilma, 2005, near Cancun, Mexico

Driving is extremely hazardous in hurricane conditions

Fog and smog

When air is full of moisture and the temperature drops, fog may occur. Fog is cloud at ground level, made up of tiny water droplets. Fog is translucent, like tracing paper, as it scatters light. Thick fog reduces visibility, and accidents on the roads, at sea, or in the air are common. Foghorns or radar locate ships and planes; traffic signals and lighthouses can guide them to safety. When fog combines with smoke, thick and dangerous smog may form.

Mask protects policeman's lungs

Pea-souper
Until the 1960s, when the Clean Air Acts forced people to use "smokeless fuel", London, England, suffered dangerously bad smog, nicknamed "pea-soupers", from the burning of coal. It caused serious breathing problems.

Take-off
During World War II, kerosene was burned to provide heat to clear fog from airport runways. The heat turned water droplets in fog into invisible vapour. It worked, but is expensive and can be dangerous.

Airport staff-member ignites fog burners

Water catchers
For residents of Chungungo village, a dry part of Chile, frequent fog is a blessing. These long, plastic fences outside the village catch water from fog that blows in from the sea, providing much of the village's water supply.

Sulphurous smog hangs over Christchurch, New Zealand

Cleaning up the air
Sulphurous smog hangs in the air above many cities. It is produced when smoke combines with fog, and is a danger to health and traffic. Today, sulphurous smogs are less common due to cleaner fuels, but equally deadly is "photochemical smog" caused by sunlight combining with air pollutants.

Gas container

Loud noise travels through this horn

Sounding the alarm

Thick sea-fog hides boats from each other. Gas released from this foghorn makes a loud noise that can be heard clearly through the fog, to help avoid collisions. Large ships have huge, deafening foghorns that can be heard over many kilometres.

Golden Gate Bridge in San Francisco, USA, is hidden beneath a blanket of fog

Fog City

San Francisco, USA, is known as "Fog City" due to its summer fog that occurs when warm, moist air meets the cool water that travels into San Francisco Bay from down the coast.

Lighting the way

Before the invention of radar, sailors had no way of seeing in thick sea-fogs. Lighthouses warned sailors of the dangers ahead, guiding ships away from rocks or shallow water, by flashing a powerful beam of light during fogs and at night.

High seas

Strong winds constantly disturb the surface of the oceans, producing waves that break on coastlines. During severe storms and hurricanes, sea water can cause flooding along the coast, and ships to sink. Scientists fear that global warming may cause more of the the ice-caps to melt, resulting in a rise in sea levels, increasing flood risks, and coastal erosion in many places.

In deep water
High seas have dangerous waves that can sink ships. Rescue helicopters help survivors, hovering above the sea while a rescuer is lowered on a winch to lift the survivors out the water.

A rescuer is lowered to the sea by a search-and-rescue helicopter

Collapsed coastal road caused by wave erosion

Tearing along
Crashing waves wreak havoc on coastlines, dissolving rock and breaking off parts of cliffs. The stormier and higher the sea, the greater the erosion. If sea levels rise, so will erosion and flood risks.

Holding back
The Thames River Barrier aims to protect London, England, from flooding until at least 2050. Ten huge gates can be raised when sea levels surge, preventing water from travelling up the river.

Tsunami
Often mistakenly called tidal waves, tsunamis are triggered by earthquakes beneath the seabed and can devastate areas, such as here on Okushiri Island, Japan.

Stormy sea
Hurricane Hugo hit the West Indies and southeastern USA in 1989 with a surge 2 m (6 ft) high. This rose to 6 m (18 ft) in some places, where the water was funnelled up along valleys.

Wall of water

Wind blows across the ocean surface, making the water swing up and down, back and forth, forming waves. When waves approach the shore, where the sea is shallower, they move more slowly, and their crests get taller and closer together. Eventually, the waves topple over, forming breakers.

This huge, plunging wave is on the verge of breaking

Snowstorms

Extremely cold conditions can endanger lives. When the temperature falls below freezing – 0°C (32°F) – snow settles on the ground. Sometimes, wind blows the snow into piles, called snowdrifts. Snow and strong winds cause blizzards, which reduce visibility. Snowflakes are clumps of ice crystals, made inside a cloud when water vapour freezes around specks of mineral dust. Ice storms occur when water in the air freezes to form icy fog at ground level.

Piled high
Snow has piled up against the side of this house in Derbyshire, England. Snowdrifts such as this form when snow carried by the wind is stopped in its tracks by an obstacle.

White-out
Blizzards have forced these drivers to stop their cars. If they remain in their vehicles, they can be found more easily, but risk freezing. One person froze to death during this snowstorm near Caen, France.

Ice crystal from a snowflake

What is snow?
The ice crystals that make up snowflakes are tiny, but their beautiful symmetrical shapes can be viewed through a microscope. Their growth depends on temperature, humidity, and air currents in a cloud. These conditions are never identical, and so no two snowflakes are the same.

Blade of a snowplough clearing a road in France

Clearing the way
Snowploughs keep major roads clear of heavy snow, and cars use tyre chains for better grip. A sudden snowfall can cause chaos; tyres easily lose their grip and accidents are common.

Frozen drips

Icicles form as water drips from ridges, such as rooftops or tree branches. A small amount of each drip freezes while the rest drips off. Gradually, drip by drip, an icicle builds up.

Wind chill

This man's face-warmer froze as he shovelled snow in Milwaukee, Wisconsin, USA. During this severe winter storm in December 1995, the temperature was -35°C (-31°F), but the "wind chill" made it feel like -70°C (-94°F). Wind chill occurs on a windy day, when heat passes from your warm body to cold air more quickly than on a calm day, making it feel colder than it really is.

Icicles hang from a cliff during an ice storm in Arizona, USA

Staying indoors

Extreme cold weather can force people to stay indoors for safety and warmth. Vehicles may become frozen, such as this car in northeast Canada, when the temperature dropped to -29°C (-20°F). During this storm, trees fell down under the weight of ice, and thousands of cattle froze to death.

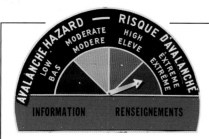

Watching for signs

Most mountain resorts warn of avalanche danger. By examining the snow, experts can tell when an area is at risk, but not where and when it will strike.

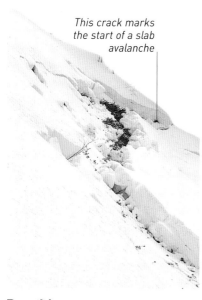

This crack marks the start of a slab avalanche

Avalanche

One of the most dangerous things in mountainous areas is an avalanche, when huge amounts of snow slide down a mountain, burying buildings and the people in them. The Swiss Alps is one of the areas most at risk, with about 10,000 avalanches every year. Avalanches occur after snow builds up on mountain slopes in layers – a new layer laid during each snowfall. When the layers are unstable, an avalanche can be triggered by strong winds, vibrations, or changes in temperature. Anybody caught under this cold, heavy blanket needs rescuing immediately.

Under cover

In areas where avalanches are common, protective sheds are often built over major roads. The sheds allow avalanches to pass over the road, keeping the road clear.

Breaking away

Most avalanches occur when melted snow breaks away as a large slab. As it begins to move, cracks (fissures) show in the snow, usually on bulging slopes and snow that's overhanging clifftops.

Snow fences protect mountain villages in Switzerland

Bang, bang

When a mass of snow is ready, an avalanche can be set off by the slightest vibration. In places threatened by serious avalanches, explosives are used to set them off deliberately, before too much snow builds up.

An avalanche forecaster checks the stability of snow layers

Snow stoppers

Sturdy trees on a mountainside can absorb some of the energy of sliding snow. Artificial barriers made of wood, concrete, or metal can provide similar protection.

Look closely

Avalanche forecasters build snow pits to examine snow layers. An avalanche is more likely if a layer contains air or is made up of graupel (ice pellets). These pellets can roll over each other, allowing slabs of snow above to break away.

Snowy river

Airborne powder avalanches, such as this one, occur soon after a fresh snowfall. They flow like water, throwing up vast splashes on the valley floor. The high-speed mass of snow smothers everything in its path, and compresses the air in front of it, creating loud tremors.

A rescue dog searches for survivors in the Swiss Alps

Sniff search

Specially trained dogs help to locate people trapped under heavy snow after avalanches. With their highly developed sense of smell, dogs are more efficient than any electronic sensor, although off-piste skiers do carry personal radio beacons.

Floods and landslides

Flooding causes more than a third of all deaths from natural disasters. A flash flood occurs when rain is heavy and rivers break their banks, or sewers quickly become overwhelmed. In the Indian subcontinent, seasonal winds called monsoons bring torrential rain and floods every summer. When torrential rain combines with high tides and strong winds, coastal areas are particularly at risk. When large volumes of rainwater mix with soil, the muddy mixture can slip down a hill – a landslide.

Noah's Ark
According to the Bible, God was unhappy with how humans were treating the world, and so decided to kill most of the human race with a 40-day flood. God chose Noah and his family to survive. He told him to build an ark and take a male and female of each species.

Damage caused by the Johnstown flash flood

Dam buster
After heavy rain on 31 May 1889, a dam near Johnstown, Pennsylvania, USA, collapsed. The north of the city was swept away by thousands of tonnes of water, and 2,209 people died.

A farmer in Java tries to save a rice crop from the floods

Rice
Monsoon rains on the island of Java, Indonesia, are vital for rice crops. But, sometimes, heavy rains bring floods that endanger lives and precious crops.

Breaking the bank
During monsoon season, the River Ganges in south Asia often bursts its banks. The floods of July and August 1998 were the worst in 20 years, submerging up to two-thirds of Bangladesh. About 1,500 people died, mostly from snakebites or waterborne diseases.

Muddy river
In May 1998, after two days of torrential rain in Quindici, Italy, local rivers burst their banks. Muddy water flooded the town, leaving 3,000 homeless and killing about 50 people – many of them buried under a thick layer of mud.

Landslide debris on a 30-m- (98-ft-) high clay slope

Watery intruder
Storm waters broke into this seaside home in Florida during Hurricane Andrew in 1991. Fierce winds and a surge of high water are caused by the low atmospheric pressure of the hurricane's centre.

Moving mud
When water and mud mix on a hillside, gravity pulls the mud and anything else in its path downwards. This hotel in Scarborough, England, slipped downhill during a landslide in June 1993.

Storm on the waterfront
These residents of Florida Keys, USA, sought refuge as Hurricane George, which had already devastated Carribean islands, hit the coastline in 1998. They battled against 140-kph (90-mph) winds and a surge of water from the Atlantic.

Home upturned by a powerful storm surge

Heat waves

A heat wave is a spell of unusually warm and humid weather. People can suffer from heatstroke – dizziness and confusion, nausea, and faster than normal heartbeats – which, in extreme cases, can kill. Sweating helps cool the body, but sweat evaporates more slowly in humid air. Despite the humidity, the land can be very dry, so wildfires are a danger.

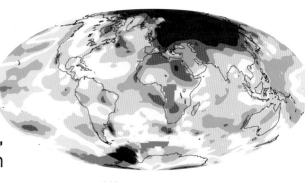

Climate change
Average temperatures are rising. In this 2008 map, orange and red show where temperatures were higher than average; areas cooler than average are blue. As temperatures rise, heat waves are becoming more common.

Urban heat islands
Temperatures in cities are usually a degree or two higher (shown in this map as yellow and white) than less built-up areas, because concrete absorbs more heat than vegetation. As a result, people in cities are at highest risk of health issues during heat waves.

Sun shade
During a heat wave, intense sunlight heats the body, increasing the risk of heatstroke and causing painful sunburn on the skin, which has similar symptoms to heatstroke. These people are using an umbrella for shade during a heat wave in Shanghai, China, in 2013.

Wildfires
In June 2012, the northwest USA experienced one of its worst recorded heat waves. Record temperatures and very low rainfall created conditions for wildfires like this one in the heavily forested state of Montana.

Europe 2003

People enjoyed the sunshine during the 2003 European heat wave. It was not all fun, though: experts estimated that the heat wave caused around 70,000 deaths, and the accompanying drought caused crop failures.

Search for food

Heat waves can cause hardship for wildlife, as wildfires destroy their habitats and food sources. This deer is searching for food in a national park near Athens, Greece, after a heat wave in the summer of 2007.

Moscow 2010

In the summer of 2010, much of Eastern Europe experienced record high temperatures. Wildfires raged for weeks in the countryside around Moscow, Russia. Smoke filled the city's air, causing smog – many inhabitants wore face masks, but the death rate in the city was twice as normal for the month.

A forest fire burning the side of a mountain in Montana, USA

Deadly droughts

Any region lacking in water due to lower-than-usual rainfall is said to be in drought. As rivers, lakes, and soil dry up, crops fail and animals starve, leading to famine among humans. Advances in medicine, transport, and communications in the 20th century allowed aid agencies to lessen the effects of water scarcity, but droughts are still a problem in much of Africa. Droughts are sometimes caused by human activities, such as over farming.

Powerful painting
This Aboriginal bark painting from Arnhem Land (a hot, dry part of northern Australia) was used in rain-making ceremonies. The stingray symbolizes the "watery" power that summons rain.

Skin and bones
Animal carcasses are a common sight during severe droughts. This unfortunate animal dried out before it had a chance to decay.

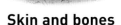

Animals gather around a waterhole in Namibia, southern Africa

Diminishing supply
Animals in dry climates gather around scarce pools of water, called waterholes. During a drought, more water evaporates and is drunk than is supplied by rainfall, and there are fewer plants for animals to eat, too. As a result, millions of animals can die during a drought.

War and want
One of the worst droughts was in east Africa during 2011 and 2012. After two years of very low rainfall, crops and livestock were severely affected. Millions of people suffered malnutrition, and tens of thousands died.

Fighting fire
Drought causes disastrous forest fires, fuelled by the dry leaves and wood of vegetation. Most fires start naturally, but some are caused by a careless act, such as a dropped match. Some trees have fireproof bark, or bark that peels off when ignited. Other trees will not germinate until their cones are scorched.

Blowing in the wind

Deserts are in permanent drought, and so most are covered in dry sand or sandy soil. The wind can blow dry sand grains around, causing sandstorms. Sandstorms create sand dunes, which make up much of the landscape of the hottest deserts.

Black blizzards

In the 1930s, the Great Plains of the North American Midwest suffered severe drought. Grasses in the fields had been ploughed, so the topsoil dried to dust and blew away in clouds. Thousands left their homes, and some died of starvation or lung disease from inhaling the dust.

Thirsty leaves

In the drylands of southwest Africa, the kokerboom tree can survive several years of drought. Its leaves shrink, having lost most of their moisture.

Cracking up

Large areas of land with no vegetation quickly suffer from drought. No plants means no water store, nor protection from winds that increase evaporation from the soil. Water helps to bind soil grains; dry mud cracks up, becomes brittle, and produces dust.

Lake Naivasha in Kenya, Africa, dried up by a drought

Polar extremes

The North and South poles are frozen all year round because they receive little sunlight. Around the North Pole, the Arctic has no land, only thick ice. Around the South Pole, Antarctica's land is constantly covered by snow. Strong winds in Antarctica are caused when cold air flows off steep slopes, blowing snow into a blinding blizzard. Temperatures peak at -40°C (-40°F) during the long, dark polar winters. The polar regions and their cold currents are important for global weather.

An icebreaker clears a path through the St Lawrence River, Canada

Breaking the ice
During winter, when huge amounts of sea ice form, powerful ice-breaking ships keep waterways clear, transport vital supplies, and are research stations.

Eye protection
Goggles protect eyes from the glare of sunlight, which is reflected by the snow.

Ice station
During summer, polar research stations house nearly 4,000 people at 42 sites. Less than 1,000 people live there in winter. By studying the weather at the poles, scientists can learn more about Earth's weather patterns.

Get a grip
A thermal lining in climbing boots, and clipping trousers to the tops, helps retain body heat in icy conditions. Crampons (spikes) on the soles provide grip.

Tough and durable plastic outer layer

Bright red colour makes the jacket stand out in a blizzard

Elasticated cuffs keep out icy winds

Spikes help to grip thick, slippery ice

Salopettes

Fly the flag
Newly fallen snow and blizzards can bury important items. Some people plant coloured flags to help them find their tents and supplies.

Pyramid tent to withstand high-speed blizzard winds

Weather station
There are automatic weather stations across the polar regions. Forecasting the weather is important for the safety of those who live and work in these hostile environments.

Undergarment traps a layer of air, which is warmed by the body

Weather balloon for gathering data about the atmosphere

Weather balloon
Equipment in this weather balloon measures the temperature. and concentration of gases in the Antarctic atmosphere. These measurements help scientists test theories and make more accurate forecasts.

Waterproof nylon outer layer with goosedown stuffing

Scientists in Antarctica use a drill to extract samples from the sea ice

Time freeze
Much of the ice at the poles has been frozen for millions of years. It preserves things that were around when it froze. By studying samples, scientists can discover what the climate was like many years ago.

Wrap up
In polar climates, "extreme cold weather outfits" cover the body. Outer layers include waterproof jacket and salopettes, made up of several layers of different materials – the best way to reduce heat loss.

Staying alive
Multi-layered gloves protect hands, which are most at risk from freezing conditions, as the body shuts off blood to them to reduce heat loss. Severe conditions can cause frostbite.

Weather watch

With enough warning that a hurricane is going to hit, many deaths can be avoided. Hurricanes can be tracked using weather satellites, but other types of extreme weather need ground-based measurements – including wind speed, temperature, and atmospheric pressure. The data are recorded using instruments around the world, on land and at sea. Forecasters use computers to analyse data and to predict how the weather will behave. The most difficult to predict are short-lived phenomena like tornadoes, and long-term conditions such as drought.

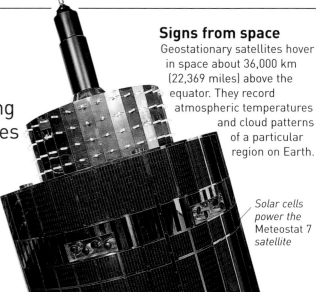

Signs from space
Geostationary satellites hover in space about 36,000 km (22,369 miles) above the equator. They record atmospheric temperatures and cloud patterns of a particular region on Earth.

Solar cells power the Meteostat 7 satellite

About 400 knobbly projections help to stabilize this balloon while in flight

Propellers sustain less damage in a storm than jet engines

Extra fuel is carried in tanks mounted on the wings

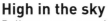
Doppler-radar dome

Round radar
Sensitive radar equipment enables weather scientists to make more accurate forecasts. The US National Weather Service relies on ground-based Doppler-radar stations to measure wind speeds and rainfall, and calculate cloud positions.

High in the sky
Balloons are essential to weather forecasting. They carry instruments into Earth's atmosphere, and transmit readings by radio. Measurements of upper atmosphere conditions are important for predicting what the weather may do next, and for discovering more about how the weather works.

Working with the weather
A modern weather forecast involves countless measurements of temperature, air pressure, and rainfall, plus complicated mathematics. No wonder computers are used – although humans are needed to interpret it all.

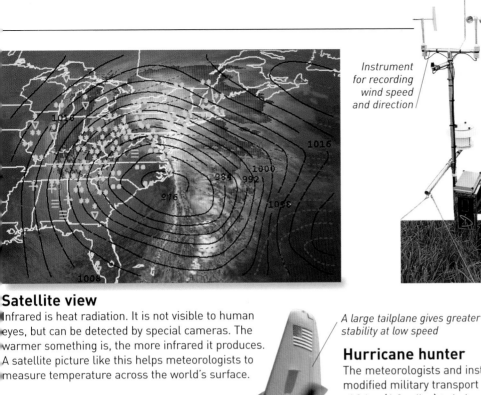

From far afield

This automatic weather station is in the middle of a field. It gathers measurements of wind speed and direction, temperature, humidity, and sunlight. The more data that meteorologists can collect, the better their forecasts will be.

Instrument for recording wind speed and direction

A meteorologist downloads weather data to his portable computer

Satellite view

Infrared is heat radiation. It is not visible to human eyes, but can be detected by special cameras. The warmer something is, the more infrared it produces. A satellite picture like this helps meteorologists to measure temperature across the world's surface.

A large tailplane gives greater stability at low speed

Hurricane hunter

The meteorologists and instruments aboard this Lockheed WC-130 modified military transport aeroplane fly into hurricanes at an altitude of 3 km (1.9 miles) to help with accurate hurricane forecasts.

Satellite is carried in the rocket's nose cone

There it goes

The Geostationary Operational Environmental Satellite system (GOES) is a series of satellites that monitor Earth's entire surface (except the regions close to the poles). This latest satellite, GOES-15, was launched on a Delta IV rocket from Cape Canaveral in 2010.

Weather buoy

Tornado pump

Weather forecasts are available across the media, from newspapers to the Internet, and petrol pumps, such as this one in the USA. A built-in screen shows tornado movements and announces warnings.

Sea search

Buoys carry automatic weather stations. They drift in the sea for weeks, measuring wind speed, temperature, and humidity. It is important to monitor sea conditions because they greatly influence Earth's climate.

Disaster relief

Extreme weather phenomena, such as storms, droughts, and floods, can cause destruction on a huge scale. When it does, people may need help to keep them alive and well, or somewhere to stay while their homes are being repaired, or even rebuilt. Food and water supplies may be affected, too. International aid agencies provide assistance, food, and medical supplies to those who suffer due to the weather.

Clean-up operation following a tornado in Connecticut, USA, October 1979

Upturned lives
A rescuer searches this upturned home following a tornado in Florida, USA. People in southwestern USA suffer many hurricanes and tornadoes, but they can never be fully prepared. While rebuilding occurs, people are temporarily housed, perhaps in a school.

Damage demolition
This building was destroyed by a tornado. The governments of wealthy countries set aside emergency funds to pay for rebuilding work. Poorer countries often need outside aid.

Portable water
During a flood, drinking water is often cut off or in short supply. This Filipino boy is collecting fresh water from a tank.

Temporary water tank provides fresh water to flood victims

Mopping up
A priority in a flood is to drain excess water. Powerful pumps clear the streets; sandbags protect properties from floodwater and control the direction of the flow.

Air meals

When a natural disaster strikes a remote location, the quickest way to bring aid is to drop supplies from the sky. Each of the tightly bound parcels from this aeroplane contained flour, oil, and canned fruit. It is difficult to drop water in these parcels, even though it is often what is most needed.

Makeshift shelters in a refugee camp in Ethiopia

Temporary homes

When drought brought famine to Ethiopia in 1989, the United Nations set up a camp in Sidamo Province, helping 45,000 people. Each family was given plastic sheeting as a temporary shelter, a sleeping mat, cooking utensils, food, and water. Refugees had to find their own cooking and building materials, putting a great strain on scarce resources.

Emergency food supplies

Disease prevention

Epidemics rapidly break out in disaster sites, and are a common cause of death. This aid worker is spraying insecticide to kill disease-spreading mosquitoes. Insecticides that will not harm people when they filter into the water supply must be used.

All dried up

When this picture was taken, there had been no rain in the Suguta Valley, Kenya, for seven years. Famine is common during a serious drought, particularly in remote areas with few supplies. This is why food aid from charities, such as Oxfam, is important.

Nature's survivors

The world's plants and animals are well suited to their environments. If they were not, they would soon die out, particularly in extreme climates such as deserts. Some living things are so well adapted to their surroundings that you may think they have been specially designed to live there. But living things adapt to their surroundings gradually – over many generations.

Feather coat
Snowy owls live in Arctic regions. Their soft, fluffy feathers hold lots of air, which insulates them against the cold. They even have feathers around their claws. If the weather becomes hot, snowy owls cool themselves by spreading their wings and panting.

Fat monster
The gila monster lives in Mexico and southwestern USA. During the warm, rainy season, food is plentiful, and the gila monster stores body fat, on which it can live during the cold, dry winter.

Fat stored in the tail provides energy in winter

Upside-down tree
According to myth, the strange-looking baobab tree angered the gods, who punished it by re-planting it upside down. In reality, the tree has leaves for only three months a year which, along with water stored in its huge trunk, enables the tree to survive East Africa's dry season.

Drip tip of a rainforest leaf

Stemming the flow
Leaves are covered with stomata (tiny holes) that allow water to escape. As it does so, more water is drawn from the soil by the plant. Where water is scarce, plants have fewer or smaller leaves. Many cacti have no leaves at all; they are simply large stems containing water.

Useful tips
In a rainforest, about 1 m (3 ft) of rain falls each month during the rainy season. Plants depend on water to survive, but constantly wet leaves kill them. Some leaves developed "drip tips", to carry the water away.

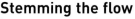

Some like it wet

Like all frogs, red-eyed tree frogs have moist skin. If their skin dries out, they will die, and so tree frogs thrive in the damp rainforests. They also have suckers on their feet to clamber among the branches.

Underground movers

Most amphibians need to keep their skin moist. During a drought, many stay in burrows, or a moist location like a rotting log. During a dry season, some frogs become dormant, cocooning themselves in moist mud.

Water hump

In the constant drought of the desert, a camel can make water from its own body fat, using a quarter of its body weight.

A camel can drink the same as a bath full of water in just a few minutes

Australian burrowing frog

In a cold climate

Emperor penguins live in the harsh Antarctic all year round. Waterproof feathers and thick fat layers help them survive on land and in the icy seas. During winter, their body fat provides an essential energy source.

Overlapping, closely packed feathers keep out fierce winds

Fluffy-feathered chicks huddle for warmth

Feet are small to minimize heat loss

Climate change

A region's climate is its typical weather over 30 years. But climates can change. Ice ages – when world temperatures are very low – cause more frozen sea water, larger polar ice-caps, and more land-ice in the form of huge glaciers. One cause of ice ages is the varying distance between Earth and the Sun. At other times, higher than normal temperatures have wiped out civilizations. Scientists use many techniques, including examining fossils or tree rings, to "read" climate records.

Ever-changing sea

The ammonoid, or ammonite, was a shelled marine animal that once lived in warm seas. Ammonoid fossils were found in Antarctic oceans, from when Antarctica was not at the South Pole, and so not cold. Like all continents, Antarctica has drifted across Earth.

Frost fair on the Thames River in London, 1813

Lost civilization

Dramatic climate change can force people out of their homes. The Anasazi civilization lived in these caves, in the southwest of what is now the USA, until about 1280. They were forced to move by a 23-year drought.

Mini Ice Age

Much of Europe experienced the "Little Ice Age", from 1500 to 1850. The average temperature was only a few degrees lower than normal, but rivers and sea water froze, and winters were harsh.

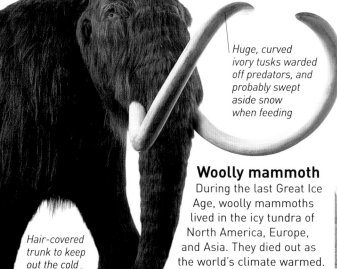

Thick, woolly coat provides insulation

Huge, curved ivory tusks warded off predators, and probably swept aside snow when feeding

Woolly mammoth

During the last Great Ice Age, woolly mammoths lived in the icy tundra of North America, Europe, and Asia. They died out as the world's climate warmed.

Hair-covered trunk to keep out the cold

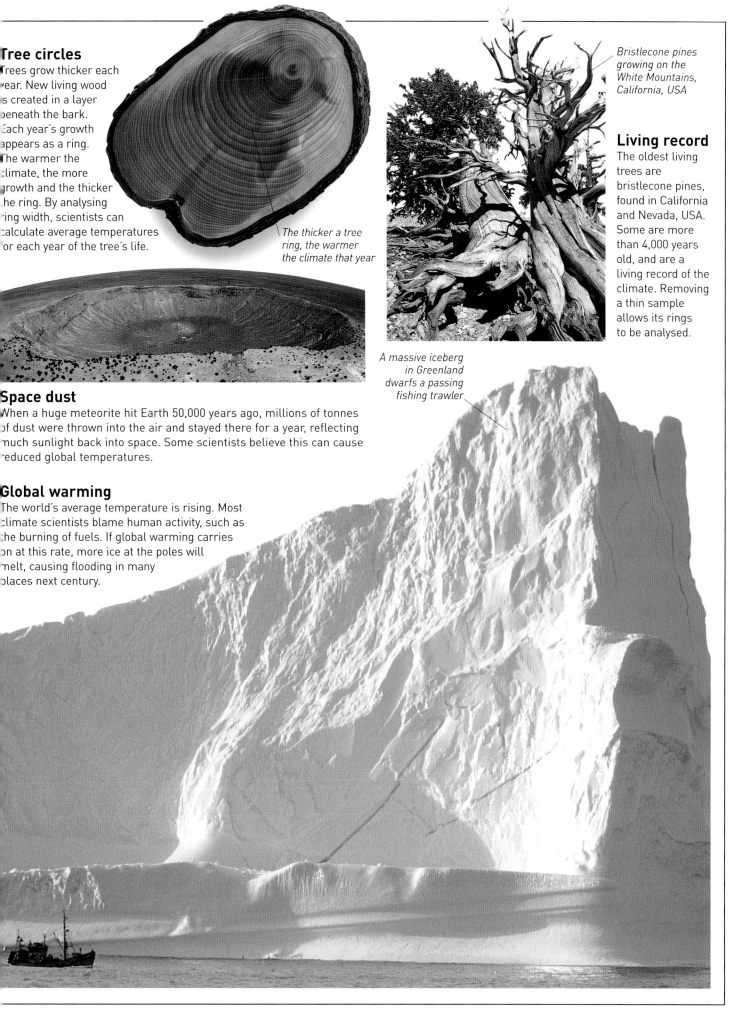

Tree circles

Trees grow thicker each year. New living wood is created in a layer beneath the bark. Each year's growth appears as a ring. The warmer the climate, the more growth and the thicker the ring. By analysing ring width, scientists can calculate average temperatures for each year of the tree's life.

The thicker a tree ring, the warmer the climate that year

Bristlecone pines growing on the White Mountains, California, USA

Living record

The oldest living trees are bristlecone pines, found in California and Nevada, USA. Some are more than 4,000 years old, and are a living record of the climate. Removing a thin sample allows its rings to be analysed.

Space dust

When a huge meteorite hit Earth 50,000 years ago, millions of tonnes of dust were thrown into the air and stayed there for a year, reflecting much sunlight back into space. Some scientists believe this can cause reduced global temperatures.

Global warming

The world's average temperature is rising. Most climate scientists blame human activity, such as the burning of fuels. If global warming carries on at this rate, more ice at the poles will melt, causing flooding in many places next century.

A massive iceberg in Greenland dwarfs a passing fishing trawler

El Niño

Every two to 10 years, part of the Pacific Ocean becomes warmer than normal during winter, and Pacific winds change direction, blowing warm water east towards South America. This El Niño effect causes extreme weather in the tropics, and can last up to four years. Outside the tropics, El Niño can cause average winter temperatures to fall and increased winter rainfall. El Niño can be predicted several months ahead, so early warnings allow farmers to alter their crops for the conditions.

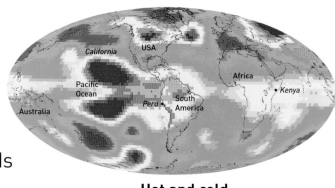

Hot and cold
This map shows how El Niño affected global temperatures in 1983. The orange and red areas show warmer than normal temperatures; the blue areas, cooler than normal.

Hard times
El Niño (Spanish for "the Christ child") was so-called by Peruvian fishermen because it appears over Christmas. When El Niño winds blow warm water over the cool Peruvian seas, plankton cannot grow in the warmer water and so the fish that eat the plankton disappear. Many Peruvians depend on fishing and so suffer during El Niño.

On the rocks
Sea lions and seabirds off the western coast of South America often starve during El Niño, as they feed on the fish that thrive on the cold-water plankton. When El Niño hits, the cool waters are pushed down, and the fish swim deeper – out of reach.

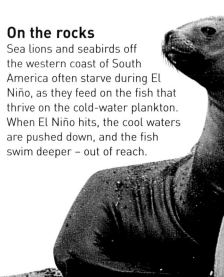

Warm and wet
The 1998 El Niño causes floods in Kenya, Africa, ruining maize crops, and spreading diseases such as malaria.

Heavy snow
During El Niño, the change in Pacific Ocean currents affects the USA's west coast. Some areas may suffer floods; others become much colder, such as with the high snow levels in the southern California mountains in 1998.

Seabed skeletons
Bleached coral indicates the presence of El Niño. Tiny algae live on coral, and are vital to its survival. They move away when the sea's temperature rises, leaving behind the coral's white "skeleton". With higher temperatures, coral reefs become barren and die.

Drought alert
El Niño reduces rainfall in Brazil, which can lead to drought. During the 1987 El Niño, Brazil's grain production fell by 80 per cent. In 1992, scientists were able to predict El Niño, and so farmers planted crops that would survive a drought.

Burning up
In 1998, El Niño brought drought to Sumatra, Indonesia. It dried the trees and forest fires burned for weeks, covering Sumatra with thick smoke. It was so dark that drivers used headlights during the day.

All dried up
During an El Niño, winds push warm water east towards South America, and away from Australia in the west. The cooler waters around eastern Australia lead to reduced rainfall, and large areas suffer from drought, causing many farmers to abandon their land.

Washed away
Much of the west coast of South America is very dry because its coastal waters are normally cool. During the 1998 El Niño, however, rain began to fall at an incredible rate. Floods broke river banks and swept away villages.

Freaky conditions

Earth's atmosphere and the Sun provide all of Earth's weather conditions. Most people experience sunshine, wind, rain, and perhaps snow, but the Sun and atmosphere can also create strange conditions. Many people have seen a rainbow, caused by sunlight hitting raindrops and bouncing back; few have seen a moonbow. Other tricks of light include haloes, mirages, and the spooky Brocken Spectre, while electric charges are responsible for the beautiful aurora lights.

Mysterious glow
St Elmo's Fire is a rare light that glows at the tips of pointed objects during an electric storm. The glow may be caused when the point leaks an electric charge that is attracted to the charge of a thundercloud.

Colours in the sky
When the Sun is low behind you, and it is raining, you may see a rainbow. Sunlight reflects off raindrops, bending as it travels through them. Each colour that makes up sunlight bends to a different angle, and so a rainbow appears as a band of colours.

A ghostly sight
Some mountain climbers see huge human figures. The figures are just the climbers' shadows cast on the bases of nearby clouds – an effect called the Brocken Spectre. The shadows may have colourful haloes called Brocken Bows.

Colours at moonrise
When a bright full Moon rises in the east and the Sun sets in the west, you may see a rare moonbow. This forms in the same way as a rainbow, so the Moon must be behind you and it must be raining in the west.

Glowing globes
People worldwide have reported balls of light that hover in midair or drift along before exploding or fading away. This ball lightning is likely electrical, caused by thunderstorms.

More snow gathers on the outside as the hollow cylinder of snow moves

Magical snowballs
When new snow falls on old and is blown by a strong warm wind, snow sometimes rolls itself up. It is rare to see them forming, but you may find a whole field full of spontaneous snowballs.

Rock reflected in the sand gives the illusion of water

Distorted view
Mirages are produced when light from distant objects bends as it passes through air at different temperatures, causing people to think they see shimmering, watery reflections in the desert.

Sun halo
When sunlight passes through cirrus (high-altitude) clouds, a halo can be seen around the Sun. Folklore suggests that haloes are a sign of imminent rain, which has some truth to it as cirrus clouds often precede rainfall.

Sunset spark
On a clear day, as the Sun sets or rises, a green flash may light the sky. It is visible only over a definite horizon, and is caused by sunlight being bent and scattered by dust particles in the atmosphere.

Auroras
These displays of coloured light can often be seen near the North and South poles. The light is produced high in the atmosphere as electrically charged solar particles are attracted towards the magnetic poles and collide with air molecules.

Beyond Earth

The Sun is a star orbited by eight planets and their moons. The Sun's radiation causes weather on Earth by heating the atmosphere. Mercury and many moons have no atmosphere, and so no wind, rain, or snow. Venus and Mars do have atmospheres; some of their weather is similar to Earth's. The gases of Jupiter, Saturn, Uranus, and Neptune swirl around as the planets spin, forming spiral storms similar to hurricanes. Further from the Sun, dwarf planets are far too cold for an atmosphere to form.

Blue Neptune
Neptune's 2,500-kph (1,553-mph) winds are the strongest in the Solar System. Methane gas in its atmosphere cools and freezes as it rises, forming white cloud bands (above).

The sky on Mars is pink during the day

The Sun is more than 100 times larger than Earth

Dust storm
Mars is covered in dust that contains iron oxide – a compound in rust – giving the planet its reddish colour. The atmosphere on Mars is much thinner than on Earth, but Mars still has fierce winds that cause dust storms.

Venusian volcanoes
Venus's surface has volcanoes, similar to Earth. Most are inactive, but when they did erupt, they spat gases into the atmosphere that play a part in the planet's weather.

Running rings

Saturn, like all the gas giants, is nearly all atmosphere, and becomes more dense the closer to the centre you go. The planet is warmed by the Sun, but in some places the outer atmosphere is still a chilly -190°C (-310°F).

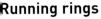

Superbolt lightning storm

High-powered winds of up to 1,800 kph (1,118 mph) encircle Saturn

Scorching storm

The Sun is a ball of extremely hot gas, increasing in heat as you head to the core. The surface is turbulent: huge storms (prominences), caused by the Sun's magnetic field, throw millions of tonnes of hot gas into space.

Storm prominence erupts on the Sun

Ultraviolet image of the Sun

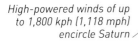

Spinning spots

Jupiter takes less than ten hours to make one rotation. This causes the planet's atmosphere to swirl, and the Great Red Spot (above). This spot is twice the size of Earth. It is a storm similar to a hurricane that has been raging for at least 330 years.

Charged up

Lightning on Earth is caused by updraughts of air in huge thunderclouds. Other planets have lightning, too. Jupiter has energetic lightning storms at its magnetic poles, which are partly caused by the planet's strong magnetic field.

Icy Europa

One of Jupiter's moons, Europa, has a thin atmosphere made up largely of oxygen. This rocky ball is coated in smooth water ice. Some space scientists think liquid water might be beneath the ice, which means life could exist in Europa's seas.

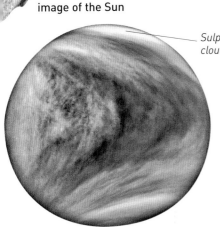

Sulphuric cloud bands

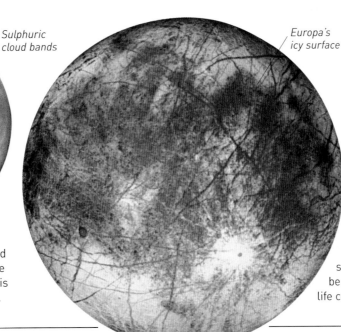

Europa's icy surface

Molten Venus

Venus is the hottest planet, shrouded in thick clouds of sulphuric acid. The atmospheric pressure at its surface is 90 times higher than that on Earth.

Did you know?

AMAZING FACTS

- Greenlanders have about 50 words for all their snow, such as "nittaalaq" (air thick with snow).

- There are more than eight million flashes of lightning every day.

- Cumulonimbus clouds can be 11 km (7 miles) tall.

The air rises quickly through the tall cloud

A cumulonimbus cloud

- 60 cm (24 in) of dry snow takes up the same space as 2.5 cm (1 in) of rain.

- On 14 August 1979, a rainbow was visible in North Wales for three hours.

- Thunder can be heard 10 km (6 miles) away from a storm, but lightning can be seen 100 km (60 miles) away.

- A temperature of 4°C (40°F) could feel like -10°C (-14°F) if there is a 72 kph (45 mph) wind blowing. This is known as the wind-chill factor.

- In storms, objects and animals can be picked up and dropped down again some distance away.

- More than 100 tornadoes have hit Oklahoma City, USA – more than any other city. Texas has more tornadoes a year – 125 – than any other US state.

- "Male" hurricanes have caused four times more damage than "female" ones since 1979 when male/female names started being used.

On 7 July 1841, hundreds of small fish and frogs fell with rain and hail on Derby, England

- Cheyenne, Wyoming, USA, is the USA's hail capital. A storm in August 1985 left 1.8-m- (6-ft-) high "haildrifts".

- Permanent snow and ice cover about 12 per cent of Earth's land.

- A lightning flash moves from the ground to the cloud at 37,000 km/second (22,990 miles/second).

- Hail falls on Keriche, Kenya, 132 days a year – more than on any other place on Earth.

- Park ranger Roy Sullivan suffered seven lightning strikes in 41 years. It set his hair on fire, injured his chest and stomach, and knocked him out.

A tornado funnel sweeps across the ground

Fork lightning

- Lightning can travel more than 10 km (6 miles), so you can suffer a strike even if there is not a storm overhead.

- Dramatic high tides result from high winds offshore and low atmospheric pressure. A 1-millibar fall in pressure causes the sea to rise by 1 cm (0.4 in); a deep depression can cause a 70-cm (28-in) rise.

- A thunderstorm can drop up to 500 million litres (110 million gallons) of rain.

QUESTIONS AND ANSWERS

The aurora borealis

Q What causes the lights known as auroras?

A Solar wind is a stream of particles flowing from the Sun's polar regions. The Earth's magnetic shield protects us from this wind, but at the poles the particles create light displays as they collide with molecules in the upper atmosphere. Near the North Pole the lights are known as the aurora borealis; near the South Pole, the aurora australis.

Q What is the blanket effect?

A At night, clouds reduce the heat that leaves Earth, keeping Earth warm. This is the blanket effect.

Q What can happen where oceans meet?

A Where oceans meet, such as off the tips of South America and South Africa, storms create huge waves. At Cape Horn, they can be 20 m (65 ft) tall.

Q What are the doldrums?

A The doldrums are a windless area of rising hot air around the equator. The rising air forms cumulonimbus clouds that produce thunderstorms and waterspouts.

Record Breakers

- In April 2011, the worst tornado outbreak in the world saw 358 tornadoes hit 21 US states in four days. Thousands were injured and 348 died.

- The lowest recorded temperature in the world is -89.2°C (-129°F), taken at Vostok, Antarctica, on 21 July 1983.

- The wettest place on Earth, with an annual rainfall of 12,000 mm (472 in) is Mawsynram, Meghalaya State, India.

- The wettest day in the world was at Foc-Foc, Ile de Reunio, Indian Ocean, where 1,825 mm (71 in) of rain fell in 24 hours.

- The windiest place in the world is Port Martin, Antarctica, where winds can average more than 64 kph (40 mph) on at least 100 days each year.

- The greatest snowfall recorded in one day was at Silver Lake, Colorado, USA, on 14 April 1921, with a fall of 1.93 m (6 ft 3 in).

Ice crystals in a snowflake

A surfer enjoys South Africa's big waves

Find out more

There are many ways to find out more about the weather. Make or buy simple weather instruments to keep a log of hurricanes and tornadoes. You could look into projects that help victims of extreme weather, or visit a wind farm to see how people harness the weather's energy.

Visit a wind farm

Wind farms use wind power to generate electricity. Visit a wind farm and discover the advantages of this renewable energy resource. Find out where it is best to position the farms.

Generator converts the movement of the shaft into electricity

The blade turns to face the wind

USEFUL WEBSITES

- To find out about the Meteorological Office, go to: **www.metoffice.gov.uk**
- For information on setting up a weather station, see: **www.metoffice.gov.uk/education/kids/things-to-do/ weather-station**
- For weather forecasts and severe weather data, go to: **www.bbc.co.uk/weather**
- To find out about people who follow hurricanes, see: **www.hurricanehunters.com**
- For tornado information, see: **www.nssl.noaa.gov/ education/svrwx101**

Monitor the weather

Build or buy your own weather centre. Keep a daily log of weather measurements, such as air pressure, temperature, rainfall, and wind speed. You or your school could join MetLink International online – run by the Royal Meteorological Society – to find out a great deal about weather around the world. You can then compare your readings with those from groups in other countries.

Hurricane crasher!

Find out how teams in the USA and Australia track hurricanes to learn more about them in trucks and planes. They take photographs and measurements, and the planes fly right into the eye of the hurricane.

Stop the desert

Find out how people, animals, and plants survive with little rainfall. In northern Africa, drought, overgrazing, and removal of trees for firewood are resulting in the expansion of the Sahara Desert. Find out about the grass-planting projects to stop the desert spreading.

Good flooring

Floods can cause damage, but they can sometimes be beneficial. They can increase soil fertility, or create an environment for wildlife. The Ouse Washes, Cambridgeshire, flood every winter, attracting thousands of migrating birds.

About 7,000 migrating swans gather on the Ouse Washes each winter

Flood warnings

Contact the environment agency to find out more about flood alerts. Check out **www.environment-agency. gov.uk** for flood information. Map your part of the country, marking flood-prone areas, and investigate why flooding is common there. Visit flood defences, too.

Places to visit

CENTRE FOR ALTERNATIVE TECHNOLOGY, MACHYNLLETH, WALES

- There are interactive displays on wind, water, and solar power, energy efficiency, green transport, and growing food organically. During school holidays, there are additional free activities. Find out more about wind farms from the wind turbine demonstration on **www.cat.org.uk**

NATIONAL SPACE CENTRE, EXPLORATION DRIVE, LEICESTER, ENGLAND

- There is information on how satellites keep an eye on the weather, and an interactive weather forecasting studio. **www.spacecentre.co.uk**

THAMES RIVER BARRIER, LONDON, ENGLAND

- Opened in May 1984, the Thames River Barrier controls floods for the River Thames. There are nine concrete piers with ten openings. Steel gates raise from the riverbed if there is high surge tide threat. Boat trips to the Barrier depart from central London and Greenwich. Visit when the barrier gates are being tested. **www.environment-agency.gov.uk/ homeandleisure/floods/38353.aspx**

WILDFOWL AND WETLANDS TRUST OUSE WASHES RESERVE, WELNEY, CAMBRIDGESHIRE, ENGLAND

- In winter, thousands of migrating ducks and swans come here, while redshanks, lapwings, and snipe breed on the reserve in summer. For more information, go to: **www.wwt.org.uk**

Glossary

ANEMOMETER An instrument for recording wind speeds.

ATMOSPHERE The gases surrounding Earth and some other planets.

ATMOSPHERIC PRESSURE The pressure from the atmosphere's weight.

AURORA Bands of light across the sky, visible near the North and South poles.

AVALANCHE A fall of snow and ice down a mountain.

BAROCYCLONOMETER An early device used to calculate the position of an approaching cyclone. It measured atmospheric pressure and wind direction.

BAROGRAPH A chart with vertical or horizontal bars showing amounts.

BAROMETER An instrument for measuring atmospheric pressure, to determine weather changes or altitude.

BEAUFORT SCALE A wind speed scale, from 0 (calm) to 12 (hurricane force).

BLIZZARD A strong, bitterly cold wind accompanied by heavy snow.

CLIMATE The usual, long-term weather conditions of an area.

CUMULONIMBUS CLOUD A billowing, white or dark-grey cloud that is very tall. Also called a thunderhead, this type of cloud is associated with thunderstorms. The top of the cloud is often the shape of an anvil, and the bottom can be quite dark if it is full of rain or hail.

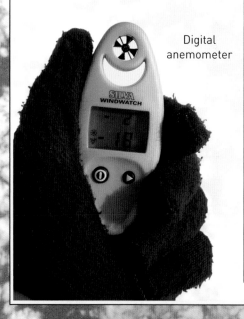
Digital anemometer

An early barometer

CYCLONE An area of low atmospheric pressure with winds spiralling in towards it – anticlockwise in the northern hemisphere, clockwise in the southern.

DEPRESSION A body of moving air that is below normal atmospheric pressure. Depressions often bring rain.

DOLDRUMS Areas near the equator with very light winds or calms.

DROUGHT A long period of little rainfall.

DUST DEVIL A strong, mini whirlwind that whips up dust and litter into the air.

EL NIÑO A warming of the eastern tropical Pacific Ocean, occurring every few years and disrupting weather patterns.

FLASH FLOOD A sudden torrent, usually caused by a heavy storm.

FLOOD When water overflows, such as from a river, and covers usually dry land.

FOG A mass of water droplets hanging in the air and reducing visibility.

GLOBAL WARMING An increase in the average temperature worldwide, believed to be caused by the greenhouse effect.

GREENHOUSE EFFECT The process in which gases absorb infrared radiation emitted by the Earth's surface, which would otherwise escape to space.

HAILSTONE A pellet of ice falling from cumulonimbus clouds that have very strong rising air currents.

HAILSTORM A storm in which hail falls.

HUMIDITY Amount of moisture in air.

HURRICANE A severe, often destructive storm, also called a tropical cyclone, and known as typhoons in the Pacific Ocean and cyclones in the Indian Ocean.

HURRICANE CHASERS People who chase after hurricanes to find out more about them.

HYGROMETER An instrument that measures moisture in the air.

ICE AGE A period of time when ice covers a large part of the Earth's land.

A meteorologist examines a rainfall monitor

ICE STORM When water in the air freezes and coats everything in ice.

JET STREAM A long current of air about 12 km (7.4 miles) above Earth's surface. Jet streams are hundreds of kilometres long, 100 km (60 miles) wide, and about 1 km (0.6 miles) deep. They can reach speeds of 300–500 kph (200–300 mph).

LANDSLIDE The slipping of a large amount of rock and soil down the side of a mountain or cliff.

LIGHTNING A flash of light during a thunderstorm, when electricity is discharged between two clouds, or between a cloud and the ground.

LIGHTNING CONDUCTOR A metal strip fixed between the highest part of a building and the ground to provide a safe route to the ground for the lightning.

METEOROLOGY The study of Earth's atmosphere, of how weather forms, and of methods of forecasting the weather.

MONSOON A seasonal wind in south Asia. In summer it blows from the southwest and brings heavy rains; in winter it blows from the northeast.

PRECIPITATION When water vapour condenses in the atmosphere and falls to Earth as rain, snow, hail, sleet, or dew.

Under the Wave off Kanagawa by Hokusai

RAINBOW An arc of colours across the sky caused by the refraction and reflection of sunlight through the rain.

SANDSTORM A strong wind that whips up clouds of sand, especially in a desert.

SMOG A mixture of smoke and fog.

SPATE The fast flow of water in a river.

STORM SURGE A dramatic high tide that may produce flooding. Caused by the sudden pressure drop and high winds of an offshore storm.

SUPERCELL A particularly large pocket of rising air that brings massive amounts of water into a thundercloud. Supercells can generate tornadoes and waterspouts.

TEMPERATURE A measurement of how hot a body or substance is.

THERMOMETER A temperature gauge, usually with a liquid column that expands or contracts in a sealed tube.

THERMOSCOPE A device that indicates variations in temperature without measuring their amounts.

THUNDERBOLT A flash of lightning accompanied by thunder.

THUNDERCLAP A loud cracking noise caused by atmospheric gases expanding rapidly when heated suddenly by lightning.

THUNDERHEAD A towering cumulonimbus cloud that is electrically charged. A thunderhead is dark in colour because it is full of rain or hail.

THUNDERSTORM A storm caused by strong rising air currents, featuring thunder, lightning, and usually heavy rain or hail.

TIDAL WAVE An unusually large wave not actually caused by the tides at all, but by an earthquake. Properly called a tsunami.

TORNADO Also known as a cyclone, a whirlwind, or a twister. A tornado is a violent storm in which winds whirl around a small area of very low pressure. There is usually a dark, funnel-shaped cloud reaching down to Earth and causing damage.

TORNADO ALLEY The name given to the parts of Kansas, Missouri, and Oklahoma, USA, that are most at risk from tornadoes.

A weather satellite

TSUNAMI A huge, destructive wave caused by an earthquake on the seabed.

VORTEX A whirling mass of liquid or gas, such as tornadoes and hurricanes.

WATERSPOUT A whirling water column drawn up from the surface by a whirlwind travelling over water.

WEATHER SATELLITE A device that orbits the Earth and send back data to help scientists forecast the weather.

WHIRLWIND A column of air whirling around an area of low pressure, and moving across the land or the surface of the ocean.

Flooding caused by monsoon rains in Vietnam

Index

Acknowledgements

Dorling Kindersley would like to thank:
Sheila Collins for design assistance.
Indexer: Helen Peters.
Illustrators: Eric Thomas and John Woodcock
Photographers: Peter Anderson, Jeoff Brightling, Jane Burton, Peter Chadwick, Andy Crawford, Geoff Dann, Mike Dunning, Steve Gorton, Frank Greenaway, Ellen Howden, Colin Keates, Dave King, Andrew Nelmerrn, Janet Peckham, Kim Sayer, Karl Shone, Andreas Von Einsiedel, Jerry Young, and Michel Zabé

For this edition, the publisher would also like to thank:
Hazel Beynon for text editing and Carron Brown for proofreading.

The publisher would like to thank the following for their kind permission to reproduce their photographs: (Key: t=top, b=below, l=left, r=right, c=centre)

Alamy Images: Paul Wood 50–51c, Reven T.C. Wurman 22–23b; **Alison Anholt White:** 14c; **Ardea London Ltd:** Francois Gohier 10bl; M. Watson 41bl; **Associated Press Ap:** 39tl, 43tl, 43b; SLF Jennings 30–31; Topham 52tr; **Bridgeman Art Library, London/ New York:** Thor's fight with the Giants, 1872 by Winge, Marten Eskil 1825–96, National Museum, Stockholm, Sweden; Plato and Aristotle, detail of the School of Athens, 1510–1511 (fresco),

Vatican Museum and Galleries 6bc; **British Museum, London:** 7ca, 7cr; **Bruce Coleman Ltd:** Jules Cowan; 57tr Jeff Foott 2b, 14–15; Johnny Johnson 55bc; Allan G. Potts 58–59b; **Corbis:** Aurora Open/ Patrick Orton 44–45b, epa/Paris Barrera 33b, Imaginechina 44cl, NASA 32bl, NOAA/CNP 32clb, Reuters/Sue Ogrocki 22tl; **Corbis UK Ltd:** 40r, 41r; Bettmann 7cr, 24crb, 42cl, 47c; Lowell Georgia 4tr, 40tl; David Muench 56cl; Galen Rowell 41cr; Dave Bartruff 68l; Bettmann 66br; Rick Doyle 65b; El Universal/ Sygma 66cl; Chris Golley 64tr; Historical Picture Archive 71l; Aaron Horowitz 64bl; George McCarthy 69cl; Sygma 68br; A & J Verkaik 66–67 bckgd; Patrick Ward 69br; Steve Wilkings 64–65 bckgd; Michael S. Yamashita 71b; **Dreamstime.com:** Khunaspix 23tr, Lastdays1 23cra, 23crb, R. Gino Santa Maria 23cr, 23crb (Saint Louis), 23br; **Sylvia Cordaiy Photo Library Ltd:** Nigel Rolstone 24–25b; **Ecoscene:** Nick Hawkes 40bl; **Environmental Images:** John Arnold 49cr; **E.T. Archive:** Guildhall Library 56cr; **European Space Agency:** 71tr; **Mary Evans Picture Library:** 24bc, 28cl, 66cl; **Getty Images:** 45tl, 45tr, AFP 45c, Boston Globe 50br, Planet Observer 32cl, U.S. Coast Guard/digital version by Science Faction 33tr; **Glasgow Museums, The Burrell Collection:** 56bl. **Scala:** Museo della Scienza Firenze 2tl, 4br, 8br, 8l, 9bl; S. Maria Novella (farmacia), Firenze 9c; **Science Photo Library:** NASA 44cr; Eric Bernard, Jerrican 38bl; Jean-Loup Charmet 24c; Jim Goodwin 52cl; Ben Johnson 36cl; Damien Lovegrove 60crb; Pete Menzel 24cl NASA. 25bc; NASA GSFC 58tr; **Glasgow Museums:** 56bl. **ICRC:** Clive Shirley 53bl; **INAH:** Mexican Museum Authority, Michael Zabe 7bl; **Kristen Klaver:** 51clb, 51bl; **FLPA – Images of**

nature: 30–31ca; J.C. Allen 26bl; D. Hoadley 20–21c; H. Hoflinger 18cr; NRC 27cl; R. Jennings 60c; S. Jonasson 13br; **Magnum:** Bruce Davidson 15ca; Steve McCurry 42bl; **Gene Moore:** 26–27, 27tl, 27cr; **N.A.S.A.:** 2tr, 2c, 4cl, 2cl, 28–29, 51br, 62tr, 62–63c, 62b, 63c, 63bl, 63br, 63t; 4bc, 16cl; Bill Hrybyk 33tc, Boeing/Carleton Bailie 51br, Robert Simmon 44tr; **National Maritime Museum, London:** 8cr; **Nature Picture Library:** Mike Lane 69cl; **Courtesy of the National Science Foundation:** 49tl, 49cla; **NHPA:** A.N.T. 19cr; **NOAA:** Dennis J. Sigrist, International Tsunami Information Centre, Honolulu, Hawaii 36b; NOAA Photo Library, NOAA Central Library; OAR/ERL/National Severe Storms Laboratory (NSSL) 23c; **Novosti:** A. Varfolomeyer 26tr; **Oxford Scientific Films:** Daniel J. Cox 48cl; Warren Faidley 4bl, 17br, 25a, 28tl; Michael Fogden 46c; Richard Henman 58bl; Mantis Wildlife Films 54cr; Colin Monteath, Hegehog House 34b; Ian West 20–21clb; Stan Osolinski 60cl; Stouffer Enterprises Inc./Animals Animals 12b; **Panos Pictures:** Trygue Bolstad 47tl; Heidi Bradner 11tr; Jerry Callow 6cl; Neil Cooper 47cb; Jeremy Hartley 46tr, 62cl; Sim Holmes 2tc, 28bl; Zed Nelson 28tr; Clive Shirley 58c, 59bc; © Tatlow 59tr; **PA News Photo Library:** EPA/Pool 14tr; **Pitt Rivers Museum, Oxford:** 7cra; **Planet Earth Pictures:** Georgette Douwma 59tl; Jiri Lochman 59cr; **John E. Purchase:** 60bl; **Rex Features:** 14cl, 30tr, 42br, 43cl, 52bl; Jean Yves Desfoux 38cl; Sipa Press 18–19; **Courtesy Of The Rosenberg Library, Galveston, Texas:** 30bl; **Royal British Columbia Museum:** 56bl.

Fraser 70r; Simon Fraser 70bl; NASA 67br; NCAR 67t; Kazuyoshi Nomachi 69tl; Claude Nuridsany & Marie Perennou 65cr; Pekka Parviainen 64tl, 65tl; Victor de Schwanberg 68–69 bckgrd; **Still Pictures:** Adrian Arbib 53br; Nigel Dickenson 52br; Filho–UNEP 59c; G. Grifiths/ Christian Aid 58clb; Olivier Langrand 54cb; Andre Maslennikor 46bc; Gil Moti 34cr; Hartmut Schwarzbach 46br, 53tr; Hjalte Tin 53cl; UNEP. 61; **Courtesy of Jeff Piotrowski/ Storm Productions Inc. USA:** 4cr, 18cl, 18clb, 18bl, 20–21tr, 20–21br; **Tony Stone Images:** 56–57b; Vince Streano 31crb; **Stock Shot:** Gary Pearl 40cb; Peter Quenault 40tr; Jess Stock 10tl, 40cl; **Sygma:** 31cra, 31br; Paul/ Pierre Pollin 39b; Claude Poulet 48tr; **Topham Picturepoint:** 20–21r; **Travel Ink:** David Toase 36tr; **University of Chicago:** 23tl; **Weatherstock:** Warren Faidley 4tl, 5tr, 10tr, 11cr, 39tl, 50bc, 51tl, 61cl, 63ct.

Wallchart credits:
Alamy Images: Reven T.C. Wurman cra; **The Trustees of the British Museum:** cla/ (Maori Kite); **Corbis:** epa / Paris Barrera clb, NASA bl, Warren Faidley cla; **Dreamstime.com:** Gentoomulmedia crb, Nickolayy tl; **Getty Images:** Photographer's Choice RF / Nacivet cl, Photonica World / Tom Stoddart cr, U.S. Coast Guard / digital version by Science Faction clb/ (New Orleans Flooded); **NASA:** NASA / JPL / Ted Stryk br; Jeff Piotrowski/Storm Productions: cb, bc, bcl (Tornado Loosing Energy); **Rex Features:** Sipa Press c

All other images © Dorling Kindersley
For further information see:
www.dkimages.com